The Last Great Banzai: Saipan, 1944

Brad Gates

The Last Great Banzai: Saipan, 1944

Brad Gates

Academica Press
Washington~London

Library of Congress Cataloging-in-Publication Data

Names: Gates, Bradley Mason (author)
Title: The last great banzai : saipan, 1944 | Bradley Mason Gates
Description: Washington : Academica Press, 2024. | Includes references.
Identifiers: LCCN 2024931205 | ISBN 9781680533248 (hardcover) | 9781680533262 (paperback) | 9781680533255 (e-book)

Copyright 2024 Bradley Mason Gates

Contents

Acknowledgments	ix
Dedication	xi
Background	xiii
Prelude	xv
Chapter 1	1
Chapter 2	5
Chapter 3	15
Chapter 4	27
Chapter 5	33
Chapter 6	35
Chapter 7	39
Chapter 8	47
Chapter 9	55
Chapter 10	63
Chapter 11	67
Chapter 12	73
Chapter 13	79
Chapter 14	89
Chapter 15	101
Chapter 16	107
Chapter 17	111
Introduction to Sources	119
Unpublished Sources	121
Published Sources	125
Personal Interviews and Letters	127
Index	133

List of Illustrations

1. The landing beach where the U.S. Marines first assaulted the island of Saipan on June 15, 1944.
2. An aerial view of the Western shore of Saipan where American forces conducted the main assault for the invasion of Saipan.
3. Soon after arriving ashore, Lt. Gen. H.M. Smith met with his staff to appraise the situation.
4. Marines take a break during a lull in the action. Mt. Tapochau looms in the background.
5. A Marine 105mm howitzer blasts away at Japanese forces to the northwest. This was the howitzer used to fire directly on the massive suicide attack.
6. A small locomotive was used, before the Japanese invasion, to haul loads of sugarcane from the fields to processing factories.
7. This train track, built to move sugar cane, was used by the Japanese to help guide their suicide directly into the artillery batteries of 3/10 during the predawn hours of July 7, 1944.
8. Dug in howitzers provided more protection for gun and crew.
9. A marine forward observer team calling for artillery fire on enemy targets.
10. Supporting arms fire devastated Garapan but infantry units still had to go in to root out small pockets of resistance.
11. July 8, 1944, witnessed the results of the terrible carnage resulting from the massive Japanese attack against U.S. Army and Marine forces the previous day. Some Japanese attackers were reportedly armed only with sticks during the attack.
12. Another picture revealing the terrible slaughter that was necessary to stop the fanatical Japanese suicide attack against American forces on Saipan.
13. This gulch was filled with dead Japanese soldiers, and at least one Japanese officer, as suggested by the officer's sword in the middle of the photo.

Acknowledgments

First of all, I have to thank Mr. Donald Chappell for inviting me to a reunion in 1984. It was the experience every young Marine dreams of when he thinks of the history of the Marine Corps. To be able to associate with those who created the heritage of the Marine Corps was an honor indeed.

All my thanks and love to my wife Kathy and our children Jarod, Alana, and Jessica for all their patience as I tried to write this work. I was not always in the best of moods when all the pieces would not go together right.

My work would not have been possible if not for the financial support of the Marine Corps Command and Staff College Foundation. Attending the 1990 and 1992 reunions allowed me to conduct the many personal interviews that were so informative.

Many, many thanks to Kerry Strong and Mike Miller at the Marine Corps Research Center. Their editing and research guidance was invaluable.

Thank-you is also in order to the staff at the Marine Corps Museum. Without their dedicated and professional assistance this book could not have been even attempted.

Special thanks to my high school English teacher, Mr. Joseph Conlon, and to many friends who always gave me moral support to keep writing.

And thanks to so many fellow Marines who encouraged and allowed me to keep working on this book.

Dedication

THIS BOOK IS DEDICATED TO THE MEN
OF THE THIRD BATTALION, TENTH MARINES,
SECOND MARINE DIVISION, SAIPAN, 1944.

I WROTE THIS BOOK AS A TRIBUTE TO THEM.

Background

On July 7, 1944 all remaining Japanese forces on Saipan conducted a suicide attack against American forces. At approximately 0300 the attackers rushed down the Tanapag Plain and into the 105th Regiment of the 27th Infantry Division. Hundreds of Japanese soldiers continued unimpeded for 1200 yards past the 105th until it ran into the 3rd Battalion, 10th Marines. Howitzer direct fire slowed but could not stop the massive suicide attack. Three of four batteries were overrun and surviving Marines held out in small pockets for nearly twelve hours until other Army and Marine forces rescued them.

In June of 1984 I was privileged to attend a reunion of the 3/10 survivors of that tremendous battle. For three days I spoke with the Marines who fought against the greatest suicide assault of World War II. I learned of the courage and heroism that happened that day.

For six years I picked up every book and article I could find about Saipan, and was disappointed to learn that every source I found gave little more than a brief over-view of 3/10's action.

As a result of that disappointment, for the next several years I dug into the military archives to study war diaries, op-plans, after-action reports, and other sources of information about the July 7th, 1944 suicide attack on Saipan. I also corresponded with many of the surviving members of the battle in order to get first- hand accounts of individual actions that day.

I wrote this book about the Saipan campaign as it was personally experienced by the Marines of 3/10. My intention is to have this book serve as a tribute to those brave men who served on Saipan in 1944.

Prelude

Lieutenant Colonel Wallace Green was not a rookie to war. The future Commandant of the Marine Corps had witnessed the aftermath of battles before, but never in his wildest dreams did he imagine what lay before him that early morning of 8 July 1944. As operations officer of the 2nd Marine Division, Green went forward to verify the reports he received of the ferocious battle on the Tanapag Plain. There on the ground before him lay the remains of hundreds and hundreds of Japanese soldiers who had participated in the previous days attack against American forces on Saipan. It was obvious to Green that in one area of the battlefield, a person could walk over a hundred yards and never touch the ground because it was possible to step from one dead Japanese to the next. In some cases, it would be necessary to step over small piles of bodies as the dead Japanese fell on top of one another. In reality such a walk would not be possible as most of the Japanese had been lying there since the previous day and the hot tropical sun already started bloating many of the corpses. Marines were still searching the area to make sure that none of their fellow Marines, who were killed in the attack, were missed and unaccounted for. It was a task that no one liked, however, no one backed away from it because every man knew that that if he were lying dead on the battlefield, other Marines would be looking for him. Some of the men participating in the search were looking for friends. But even though they previously knew a man, as a result of wounds and the severe effects of the sun, it was often difficult to easily identify the killed Marines.[1]

Arriving from the rear were bulldozers that dug long trenches used for mass graves for the dead Japanese. The dead Americans were taken south to be buried in the division cemetery. Besides those killed and those wounded severely enough for immediate evacuation, many remained who

---

[1] General Wallace M. Greene Jr., USMC (Ret.), Telephone interview, November, 1990, McLean, Virginia.

could only shake their heads and wonder. Some cried, some just sat silent, but all reflected on the past 24 hours and what they had endured. They just survived the largest Japanese suicide attack of World War II. As the artillerymen of 3/10 collected their thoughts, many asked themselves "Why?" However, that early morning very few of them recalled their thoughts of eight months earlier when they were upset and asking the question, "Why not?" Little could they have known eight months prior at Tarawa, what the future held for them at Saipan on 7 July 1944.[2]

---

[2] Multiple interviews at reunions of Third Battalion, Tenth Marines, 1990 and 1992, Dubuque, Iowa.

Chapter 1

They had joined the Marine Corps to kill Japanese, not sit on a ship in the ocean. But during the intense fighting of Tarawa the men and howitzers of the 5th Battalion, 10th Marines were not sent ashore. The tiny island of Betio was a fierce struggle as a well dug-in Japanese force successfully denied the assaulting 2d Marine Division a beachhead large enough to get ashore the 105 millimeters howitzers of 5/10. Although the island was over 4000 yards long, its width was less than 1000 yards across the axis over which the Marines had to attack. Little by little as the Marines were able to achieve a beachhead, the smaller pack 75 howitzers of the 1st Battalion, 10th Marines did land to give infantry regiments much needed fire support as they gutted their way across the barren expanse of sand and dead bodies.[1]

At one point during the Marines' assault on Betio the situation was bad enough ashore that the artillerymen of 5/10 were told to make preparations to land as a rifle battalion. According to Major General Julian Smith, the commanding general (CG) of the division, "...consideration was being given to a plan to organize the support group into provisional battalions."[2] Upon hearing this the men took their carbines out on the weather deck of their ship to begin snapping in with their weapons. This made Captain Frank Huston of "O" Battery very happy since he had been pressing all day to get into the melee ashore. However, as the situation ashore improved that was not to happen. The artillery Marines were disappointed that they did not get to land on Betio because, like any Marine unit, they wanted to be in the thick of the fight. But this time it

---

[1] Martin Russ, Line of Departure: Tarawa (Garden City, New York: Doubleday, 1975), p. 111.
[2] Lieutenant General Julian C. Smith, USMC (Ret.), Marine Corps Oral History Collection, Archives Branch, Marine Corps Research Center, Marine Corps University, Quantico, Virginia.

wasn't to be; not this time anyway.[3]

On the second day of the Tarawa battle some of the artillerymen were tasked to assist in the not-so-glorious job of collecting the bodies of their fallen comrades who were floating in the water or being pushed up onto the beach. Many of the fallen Marines were killed early on D-day and by the afternoon of the second day it became obvious that something must be done. Using small boats from their ship the Marines moved toward the beach and shallow water where they collected the floating bodies of the fallen Marines. After the men were recovered from the water they were taken out to the larger ships and carried on board. After identification was made the body was placed in a burial bag and a five-inch shell from the ship was fastened to the sack and the Marine was buried at sea. No one argued that it was no way to treat a man who gave his life for his country, but the circumstances left no other options. There was no way of getting the bodies back to the states quickly, and the ships had inadequate facilities to care for the dead on the long voyage home. Taking the bodies ashore for burial on the second day was also out of the question as the battle raged on, and what the outcome would be was still in doubt. Finally on the 4th day as the island was secured the Marines who died were laid to rest in the division cemetery.[4]

In addition to the Marines who died on Betio, there were thousands of Japanese in need of interment. Marine working parties were assigned to gather the bodies of the dead Japanese and place them in large trenches dug to serve as mass graves. Private First Class (PFC) William Miller of "O" Battery was one of the men assigned to the Japanese burial detail. In the hot tropic weather, it did not take long for a body to begin to bloat and start to decompose. PFC Miller and the other Marines obtained six feet lengths of heavy communication wire, and this wire would be wrapped around the ankles of the dead enemy to drag them to the grave site. As they arrived at the large trench the men would walk down into the trench and as they walked past the previous body would simply drop the wire and walk out the other side.

---

[3] Harold A. Lane, "Recollections of the 10th Marines," March 1990, Santa Rosa, California, p.5.
[4] Wilber J. Buss, Letter to author, May 18, 1990, Lake Elsinore, California.

The Japanese had lots of time to prepare their Tarawa defenses, and as a result there were many, many bunkers on the island. Many of the enemy soldiers were killed inside bunkers and had to be removed. Because of the fanatical nature of many of the Japanese soldiers, certain precautions were taken prior to attempting the removal of anything from bunkers. According to Miller, there was a required procedure to throw a hand grenade into every bunker prior to going in to get any bodies. This procedure was to assure that there was no enemy soldier hiding inside intent on killing one last Marine before he died. Although it was definitely an unpleasant task to bury the enemy, it had to be done and the Marines always do what has to be done.[5]

After the Tarawa campaign ended, the men of the 2d Marine Division hoped and expected that they would be heading back to New Zealand where the division had gone to rest and recuperate after Guadalcanal. It was at Pahautanui, New Zealand that 5/10 was activated on 14 June 1943. Major William Crouch was the first commanding officer until the senior major, Howard V. Hiett, assumed command on 29 July and Major Crouch became the Executive officer.[6] New Zealand had been a great place to train even if the weather was extremely cold at times. But it was not the great training that the men looked forward to as much as it was the great liberty. The 5/10 Marines camp was located at Pahautanui. It was a nice place and close enough to Wellington that the men enjoyed their liberty in the capitol city of New Zealand. The city had several theatres, and PFC Dodd Sellers enjoyed spending one evening in the Kings Theatre watching the movie "Belle Starr" and paying three pence for a Coca Cola.[7] The people of New Zealand were friendly toward the Marines and many of the young single men thoroughly enjoyed spending their pounds and shillings on the young ladies. Lieutenant Jim Brandt of 5/10 fell in love with and married a lovely girl from New Zealand, as did many others. About the only bad taste that the Marines acquired in New Zealand was for the taste of mutton. With an over-abundance of sheep in the land, the

---

[5] William J. Miller, Interview with author, September 1992, Dubuque, Iowa.
[6] Ralph W. Donnelly, Brief History of 3d Battalion, 10th Marines December 1972, Headquarters, United States Marine Corps, Washington, D.C.
[7] Dodd Sellers, "As I Recall: Remembering 1941-1946," March 12, 1991, Tuscaloosa, Alabama, p. 11.

men found themselves eating mutton over and over again to the point where many hoped they would never see it again.[8]

On 27 November, 5/10 found that the ship it was on, the USS ORMSBY, was departing the waters off Tarawa and within a very short time it was confirmed that their ship was not heading to New Zealand. Instead, the Marines of Major General Julian Smith's Second Marine Division were steaming towards the Hawaiian Islands. The long trip to Hawaii was not a pleasant one. Many of the berthing areas were used as sickbay facilities therefore places for the men to relax or sleep were limited. Even the berthing areas available for the men to sleep were very uncomfortable as the heat of the tropics made the ships very warm and the ventilation was poor at best. Every day there were more burials at sea and the smell of death lingered. As more of their fellow Marines died the men of 5/10 felt a greater sense of remorse that they had not been sent into the great battle which just occurred. Many felt that they were not deserving of the star for the Tarawa campaign that would be authorized for their Asiatic-Pacific ribbon.[9] Throughout the trip the men passed the time as best they could.

At different times men would attempt to assist the medical personnel caring for the wounded, but there was usually little they could do. The usual pastimes of reading, card games, and talking about their girls were common amongst the men. Standing out on a weather deck and just gazing at the ocean or watching the flying fish also occupied time for most men.[10] Some of the men in the artillery battalion befriended a few of the Korean prisoners captured on Tarawa. These Korean men were laborers the Japanese had brought to the island to work as virtual slaves, so there was no animosity toward them from the Marines. The time on ship between New Zealand and Hawaii would be a long stretch. In addition to the inconvenience of little space to live in, the food aboard ship was strictly rationed and the men were always hungry. For entertainment the only movie the ORMSBY had was The Yellow Rose of Texas and it was played over and over again. By the time the ship arrived at Pearl Harbor the Marines had all practically memorized Gene Autry's lines.[11]

---

[8] Lane, "Recollections," p. 4.
[9] Ibid., p. 5.
[10] Anthony Zito, Letter to author, December 1, 1990, Forrest Hills, Pennsylvania.
[11] Sellers, "As I Recall," p. 22.

Chapter 2

Most of the men thought that going to Hawaii would not be too bad. But when the ships arrived at Pearl Harbor early on 9 December and the men weren't allowed off, they wondered what was going on. In addition, many of the men had never been at Pearl Harbor before and as they viewed the top of the USS Arizona, they all felt a strong sense of emotion. Another factor that caused some anger was the handling of the Korean laborers by the military police as the supposed prisoners were being taken off the ship. As a few of the men on the ship observed the excessively rough handling of their Korean friends, some intense threats towards the military police corrected the situation. Soon the Marines found their ships leaving Pearl Harbor and the island of Oahu as they began moving to the big island of Hawaii and its port of Hilo on the Eastern shore. Here they began their offload, still not exactly sure what to expect.[1]

Hilo was not a port city with sufficient docks and piers to accommodate all the large warships that transported the 2nd Marine Division. However, the Navy and Marine Corps were somewhat experienced at getting Marines ashore even though no proper facilities were available. LST's (Landing Ship - Tank) beached themselves and the larger deep draft ships used their smaller landing craft to get the men and equipment ashore. After the artillerymen assembled their howitzers, trucks, and other equipment at Hilo, the word came down to prepare to move out. As some of the convoys moved out along the coast road, other convoys left Hilo and headed inland. Quickly they realized that the road they were traveling on was mostly uphill. For 10, 20, 30 miles the artillery battalion continued its climb uphill and inland toward the center of the large island. Just off the ocean, at the lower altitudes where the climate was dry, the vegetation was green and sparse, but as the Marines got higher

---

[1] Multiple interviews at reunions of Third Battalion, Tenth Marines, 1990 and 1992, Dubuque, Iowa.

onto the mountain the terrain leveled off and became miles and miles of grassy meadow. As they continued inward the men could not help but notice two prominent land features on the island. To the south was the volcano peak of Mauna Loa and to the north was the volcano peak of Mauna Kea. As the convoys continued along the bumpy road that led between the two volcanic peaks, they were surprised by how abruptly they left the green pasture and entered the barren lava beds the two volcanos created many, many years earlier. For over ten miles the Marines traveled through the lava beds. After turning northward and passing west of Mauna Kea the road finally left the volcanic rock and reentered the vast area of lush green pasture. Finally, over 65 miles from Hilo and almost 6,000 feet higher, the convoys stopped near the small village of Kamuela. Kamuela was the field headquarters of the huge Parker cattle ranch and it was here that Major General Smith had established his division command post the previous evening at 1800.[2] This would be the home of the 2nd Marine Division in the months ahead.

The Parker Ranch was nearly a century old when the Marines arrived in December 1943. In the mid-1800s, John Palmer Parker of Massachusetts traveled through the Hawaiian Islands and realized the tremendous potential of the vast expanse of land. Parkers's initial purchase of land was only a few hundred acres, but over the years the Parker Ranch grew until it was nearly a half-million acres. The cattle herd on the ranch was estimated to be about 35,000 Herefords, which were under the watchful eye of 250 cowboys and other hired hands of the ranch.[3] One of these cowboys told Corporal Charlie Klotz of Roaring Spring, Pennsylvania, that the vast expanse of land was so great that occasionally a ranch cowboy would find a cow that died of old age and was never branded. It was born and spent its entire life out on the open range high in the Hawaiian mountains.[4] Many of the Marines were overwhelmed by the vastness of the ranch and its huge herds of cattle. Some of them who dreamed of being a cowboy when they grew up must have thought they

---

[2] War Diary, Headquarters, Second Marine Division, Fleet Marine Force, January 12, 1944, In the Field.
[3] Tarawa Boom De-Ay, Published By And For The Men Of The Second Marine Division, Number 1, Volume 1, January 6, 1944, Camp Tarawa, Hawaii.
[4] Charles Klotz, Interview with author, June, 1989, Roaring Spring, Pennsylvania.

were in heaven.

Just after arriving at their new camp the artillerymen learned they were getting a new regimental commander. The previous commander, Brigadier General Bourke had not accompanied the regiment into the mountains of Hawaii. He was transferred to a new assignment as assistant division commander of the newly forming 5th Division at Camp Pendleton, California. Later in the war General Bourke would become the commanding general of the 5th Marine Division and lead it in the invasion of Okinawa. On 9 December 1943, command of the 10th Marine Regiment was assumed by Colonel Raphael Griffin. Colonel Griffin was a graduate of Virginia Military Institute and had 27 years in the Marine Corps. His nickname was Bulldog, but according to Brigadier General George Shell, who was the commanding officer (CO) of 2d Battalion, 10th Marines (2/10) in 1943, the nickname was definitely not a reflection of Colonel Griffins disposition as he was one of the nicest men anyone would ever want to meet. Colonel Griffin had commanded the regiment from 1938 to 1940, so the artillery of the 2d Marine Division was in experienced hands.[5]

Most people think of the Hawaiian Islands as warm and green, but in December at 6,000 feet that was not what the Marines were thinking. During the day when the sun was shining the weather and temperature were very pleasant, but as the sun went down so did the temperature. Lieutenant Wilber Buss, the 5th Battalion communications officer, was born and raised in Edgemont, South Dakota. He was one of those men who made the assumption that Hawaii would be nice and warm, but according to Buss, "Hawaii was the coldest damn tropical island in the world."[6] Apparently there was good reason for choosing the cooler climate of the Parker ranch for the 2d Division to recuperate. Many of the men still suffered from the effects of malaria they contracted on Guadalcanal and medical authorities believed that the cooler climate would be beneficial to their recuperation.[7] While the cool climate was helping the malaria

---

[5] David N. Buckner, Major, USMC, A Brief History Of The 10th Marines, History and Museums Division, Headquarters, United States Marine Corps, 1981, Washington, D.C. p. 68.
[6] Wilber J. Buss, Letter to author, 18 May,1990, Lake Elsinore, California.
[7] Richard W. Johnston, Follow Me-The Story of the Second Marine Division in World War II, (New York: Random House, 1948), p. 166.

problem, it was also creating some very cold and uncomfortable nights for the men attempting to sleep without a sufficient number of blankets. Corporal Ollie O'Dell vividly remembers the cold nights and how he and other Marines would sleep in their heavy overcoats in an attempt to keep warm.[8] So it was high up on the big island of Hawaii, almost in the shadow of Mauna Kea, that the 2d Marine Division would establish a camp in which to rest and heal after the Tarawa Operation. It was also the place where the Marines would refit and train for their next operation, wherever that was to be.

Although the Marines had no way of knowing it, December of 1943 was when the Joint Chiefs of Staff were busy discussing what would be the next major U.S. objective in the Pacific. Over the objections of General MacArthur, the JCS agreed with Admiral King that the next target for the Marines would be the Marianas. King explained that the three major islands of the Marianas (Saipan, Tinian, and Guam) would provide the needed bases for operations against Luzon, Formosa, and the Japanese mainland. In addition, possession of these islands would outflank the Jap bases in the Carolinas and therefore could force a desired showdown with the Japanese at what would be the limit of their range from their land bases in the Southwest Pacific. The Army Air Force also liked the idea of capturing the Marianas since that would put mainland Japan within reach of their long-range bombers.[9]

However, the Pacific Theater of Operations strategy being discussed in Washington was not foremost on the minds of the men at Hawaii. The immediate problem for the Marines of 5/10 and the rest of the division was to build a camp. Already there and laid out in neat rows was the wood and tentage that the men would sleep in. The tents were called pyramidal tents because of the shape of their tops. Each of these tents slept eight men. Each tent was erected on a wooden platform by the men who slept in it, and working parties erected the common areas such as supply, motor sections, and mess tents. As time went on, some semi-permanent buildings were set up on concrete decks for galleys and mess halls. In

---

[8] Faye O'Dell, Letter to author, Date unknown, Perry, Oklahoma.
[9] Henry I. Shaw Jr., Bernard C. Nalty, and Edwin C. Turnbladh, History of U.S. Marine Corps Operations in WW II Central Pacific Drive, Vol. III (Washington: Historical Branch, G-3 Division, Headquarters, U.S. Marine Corps, 1966). p. 236.

specific areas of the camp large pits were dug deep enough to accommodate the "ten-holer" that was placed over it. Shower tents were also constructed to enable the men to take a fresh water shower, something they were not able to enjoy while on the ship.[10] The only problem was that the only water available for showers was cold water. For this reason, the Marines tried to get their showers in during the day, but that was not always possible. Complicating the coldness of a night shower was the fact that it took a while to get a light hung in the shower tents. This particular problem caused an embarrassing moment one evening for PFC Tony Zito of Forest Hills, Pennsylvania. Zito and several of his buddies entered the showers one night for a much-needed shower. That night the water must have felt a little colder and Zito proceeded to express his dissatisfaction about it. After bitching about the water, he directed his anger toward the officers because he suspected that they were probably enjoying nice hot showers in lighted tents. After leaving the shower tent and moving into the drying and dressing area Zito still had a few choice words of displeasure to express about the water and the officers. It was just about then that another man who had been in the shower turned on the flashlight he had with him. The small amount of light that the flashlight provided was just enough to reveal to the men in the tent that its owner was the executive officer of 5/10, Major Hitt. It is doubtful that Major Hitt heard or cared about the quick apology that Zito was spitting out since the XO and other men in the tent were laughing so hard and loud at the time. All of Zito's buddies enjoyed that story for a long time afterward.[11]

As the camp was being constructed a working party was formed to build a brig. Already there were men who had been assigned time in the brig for various infractions, but there was no brig in which they could serve their time so one had to be built. PFC Rod Sandberg was a member of the working party that built the Camp Tarawa brig. The structure was built of wooden planks and contained twenty cells about 8'x 4'. There was also a large room where the brig rats stowed their personal belongings while they were in the brig. Taking part in constructing the brig had a special

---

[10] Multiple interviews at reunions of Third Battalion, Tenth Marines, 1990 and 1992, Dubuque, Iowa.
[11] Anthony R. Zito, Letter to author, 12 January, 1990, Forest Hills, Pennsylvania.

significance for Sandberg because when it was completed, he stowed his personal gear in the big room and then proceeded to occupy one of the cells for the next twenty days. Although the diet of the men in the brig was to be bread and water (or piss and punk as the men called it), it was not uncommon for sympathetic guards to slip in a little pogey bait now and then.[12]

Construction of the camp was progressing and it was only days after the Marines arrival that the camp was named Camp Tarawa, in honor of the battle where the division had displayed such valor. Exactly one week after they arrived a 2d Division Training Memo was published to direct training for the rest of December. Division Training Memo 108-43 of 16 December directed that the period of 15 - 31 December be utilized for: a. Shakedown, b. Physical conditioning, & c. Individual training.[13] Shakedowns were not uncommon to the Marines since every so often the officers would inspect the troops' gear to make sure that a Marine was not trying to keep an unauthorized souvenir. Items such as enemy weapons were the focus of most inspections.

By the third week in December Camp Tarawa was shaping up, and even though there is no place like home for Christmas, Camp Tarawa started preparations to make Christmas of 1943 as enjoyable as it could under the circumstances. Christmas worship services were conducted at many different locations throughout the camp. Some Marines were able to attend services at a chapel in the adjacent village of Kamuela, many worshipped in tents, and one chaplain conducted his Christmas service in an unused horse stable.[14]

Many of the Marines had been skeptical a few days before Christmas when they first heard rumors that they would get a real turkey dinner for Christmas. But all doubts were removed as the aroma of turkey permeated the air around the mess tents that Christmas day. Even though it was not Moms' cookin', the Marines were served up a fine Christmas dinner with all the fixin's. The Camp Tarawa menu listed the following items:

---

[12] Rod Sandberg, "Battery "O" 5th Bn.," Date unknown, Bixby, Oklahoma, p. 7.
[13] War Diary, January 12, 1944.
[14] "Tarawa Boom De-Ay," January 6, 1944, Number 1, Volume 1.

Fruit Punch, Stuffed Celery and Olives, Celery Hearts and Sweet Pickles, Candy and Nuts, Jello Salad with Mayonnaise, Roast Turkey with Raisin Dressing, Giblet Gravy, Sweet Potatoes, Irish Potatoes, French Peas, Pumpkin Pie, Mince Pie, Fruit Cake, Brandy Hard Sauce, Coffee, Milk, Bread and Butter.[15]

In addition, men were to drink their first stateside beer in a long time.

On 24 December Major General Smith made a Christmas address to the men of his division in a crowded camp ball park. He passed on the laudatory remarks of praise he had received from senior Marine and naval officers; but it is doubtful that anything he said that day was as inspirational as his closing remarks when Gen Smith said, "It will always be a source of supreme satisfaction and pride to be able to say - I was with the Second Marine Division at Tarawa."[16]

The holiday season was accompanied by the announcement of a division recreation program. Transportation was being coordinated for trips down to Hilo for swimming and fishing. Also, to be available were tours on glass-bottomed boats. Within the confines of Camp Tarawa organizational athletics were being formed. Softball, baseball, and basketball leagues were starting up and a boxing smoker was being planned.[17] Like the other battalions, each battery in 5/10 had a basketball team. Playoffs were conducted within the battalion, and then within the 10th Marine regiment before sending the winning artillery team to the division playoffs. One of the highlights of the basketball season involved acquiring a pair of shoes for PFC Gilbert McElroy. PFC McElroy was affectionately known as "Feets" because he wore a size 15 shoe. The closest shoes to be found were the size 13's of the battalion executive officer, Major Hitt. Being a good officer and not wanting to deprive a Marine the opportunity of playing basketball, Maj Hitt gladly loaned his shoes to PFC McElroy. Even though they would be tight, McElroy felt they would work as he put his feet into the Major's shoes. It wasn't long,

---

[15] Christmas Dinner Program, Fifth Battalion, Tenth Marines, December 1943, Camp Tarawa, Hawaii.
[16] "Tarawa Boom De-Ay," January 6, 1944, Number 1, Volume 1.
[17] Ibid.

much to PFC McElroy's terror, before his feet were sticking out of the ripped canvas tennis shoes of the battalion executive officer. The basketball program was to build morale, and the other Marines had great fun building their own morale at PFC McElroy's expense as they assured him he was in big trouble for tearing Major Hitts shoes.[18] Naturally, that was not the case.

    All of the activities planned for the Marines were to serve as a boost for their morale. But without a doubt the biggest morale booster for a Marine away from home is a letter from family back in the States. While at Camp Tarawa the mail was eagerly received every day. It was on Hawaii that PFC William Miller and Lieutenant Harold Lane of 5/10 learned that each had become a first-time father.[19] Receiving mail from home was easier than sending it home as all outgoing mail had to censored to be sure that no one accidentally gave away information they should not. Regulations stated that telling of personal experiences was authorized, but no mention was to be made of ship movements, dates, casualties, tactics, troops, ships involved, or any information that may be of value to the enemy. The battalion officers were assigned the duty of reviewing the men's outgoing mail. The battalion intelligence officer, Captain Gavin Young, was responsible for reviewing the outgoing mail of officers.[20]

    Liberty from Camp Tarawa was nothing to get very excited about. Especially when compared to the liberty they had enjoyed in New Zealand. The tiny town of Kamuela had a USO, a theater, a skating rink, a couple of places to eat, and a couple of bars. Unfortunately, there were too many Marines for the facilities to accommodate. Liberty runs into Hilo required a long, bumpy, dusty ride down the mountain. Some of the men were known to carry a change of clothes with them so after arriving in Hilo they could shower off the heavy road dust from the trip and put on clean clothes in order to better enjoy their liberty. The USO's always made a great effort to entertain the men, but when there are lots of Marines and not too many girls it is not a good place for liberty. However, there were other places on the island where the Marines could pull liberty. PFC Fayette Ellis enjoyed

---

[18] Harold A. Lane, "Recollections of the 10th Marines," March 1990, Santa Rosa, California, p. 8.
[19] Lane, Recollections, p. 6.
[20] Gavin Young, Interview with author, September 1992, Dubuque, Iowa.

going to the town of Honikau on the East coast between Kamuela and Hilo. There, located high on a cliff overlooking the ocean, was a nice restaurant where Ellis enjoyed eating. Adjacent to the restaurant was a photography studio where many of the Marines had pictures taken to send home to loved ones.[21]

---

[21] Fayette Ellis, Letter to author, February 18, 1992, Irving, Texas.

Chapter 3

As the new year began, Major General Smith and his staff were pleased with the progress of the 2d Marine Division and Camp Tarawa. On January 6, 1944, the division published its first edition of the Tarawa Boom De-Ay, the weekly newspaper of the 2d Marine Division. The newspaper was eight pages long and covered all the news of the division, as well as the highlights of world news and the war in the European Theater of Operations. Many of the men had friends and family members serving there. The paper also had extensive coverage of the division sports program. Tarawa Boom De-Ay even had its own comic strip entitled MALE CALL. Feature character of MALE CALL was the lovely Miss Lace, the heartthrob of all who saw her.

In the first edition of the paper was a printed message from the Commanding General to his division.

A WORD FROM THE GENERAL

To the Officers and Men of the Second Marine Division:

The beginning of the New Year, when our Division is again assembled in one camp, is an auspicious time to inaugurate the publication of a Division periodical.

In spite of the dispersion of the units of this command in the past, a remarkable spirit of unity has obtained, which I believe will be furthered by the systematic dissemination of news from the various organizations of the Division.

The Second Marine Division, under the guidance of divine Providence, has made an enviable record during the less than three years of its existence. It has participated in two major engagements that have given the nation the names Guadalcanal and Tarawa to stand beside the Halls of Montezuma and the Shores of Tripoli.

It has been attached to two Amphibious Corps and has

added luster to the fame of each. It has been stationed on the territory of an allied nation and by its conduct has built up a spirit of cooperation and friendship that will be lasting and mutually beneficial to our respective nations. All in all, the Second Marine Division has lived up to and added to the traditions of the Marine Corps in peace and in war.

For the New Year, the record of our past performances must serve to inspire us to even greater achievements. We must continue on the road to decisive victory in order that our country may again enjoy the benefits of peace and security.

JULIAN C. SMITH
Major General, U. S. M. C.

General Smith had plenty of good reasons to provide inspiration and challenge to his men for he knew full well the demanding tasks that lay ahead.

The new year for the Second Marine Division brought with it the official approval and adoption of the new insignia. On the background of a scarlet shield was a hand holding a gold torch with a number 2 on it. Around the hand-held torch were five stars representing the Southern Cross. The new division insignia was to be worn one half inch below the seam on the left sleeve of the service uniform.[1]

Unbeknownst to many of the Marines in the 2d Division, the adoption of an official division patch did not occur without a couple of mix-ups along the way. The first patch believed to exist was the unauthorized design. This patch was a diamond shaped blue background trimmed in white. Just inside the white were the five stars of the Southern Cross, and in the center was a red snake shaped somewhat like a 2 with the word GUADALCANAL in gold letters on it. This patch was observed being worn in San Diego, Ca. in September of 1943. Supposedly a senior officer in the area had a picture taken of the patch and sent to Gen Smith who replied that he had never seen the "...so called coral snake patch..." It is believed that the patch was manufactured at the request of 2d Division

---

[1] "Tarawa Boom De-Ay," Published By And For The Men Of The Second Marine Division, 1: 1, January 6, 1944, Camp Tarawa, Hawaii.

veterans returning from Guadalcanal. Some veterans of the 2d Division believed that this patch design was rejected because it looked very similar to the patch of the 1st Division.

The second mix-up in creating a 2d Division patch was caused by the appearance of an incorrect drawing of the official insignia in a colored insert of the Headquarters Bulletin in January of 1944. The incorrect drawing was caused by a misunderstood description of the insignia. A 2d Division veteran was describing the insignia over the phone to the editor of the Headquarters Bulletin and described the shield as being heart shaped. So, after the incorrect picture appeared a private manufacture produced the patch as it incorrectly appeared in the Bulletin.[2]

The tasks ahead of the division would undoubtedly be long and arduous, therefore demanding much preparation and training. Guidance for the training that the Marines would undergo in the new year was published on December 30, 1943, in Division Training Order Number 33-43. The first paragraph stated that future combat operations were expected to be conducted against defended atolls, generally similar in type and climatic conditions to Tarawa. It then went on to advise organizational commanders that from time to time classified "Operation Memoranda" will be issued to acquaint units, as far in advance as possible, with pertinent details which should be incorporated in the organizational training program.

Paragraph 2 of the training order provided the general plan for training. It stated that the initial training was to prepare the division for amphibious training by March 1,1944. The training week would be a seven-day week, however one day per week would be directed as a liberty day as designated by a Camp Special Order. The training being conducted would be broken down into 2 phases. Phase I was to run from January 1st to February 15th inclusive. During this phase the training was to be devoted to organizational training, however infantry regiments were instructed to conduct combined exercises with artillery and tank units whenever practical.

Phase II of the training would be from February 16th to March 1st

---

[2] Smith & Pelz, Shoulder Sleeve Insignia of the U.S. Armed Forces 1941-1945, (Erin, Tennessee: R.W. Smith, 1981), p. 191.

inclusive, and be devoted to combined training in accordance with Division directives to be issued at a later date.

Paragraphs a. through e. of the detailed plan of the training order were applicable to all units. True to form in the Marine Corps, the first training requirement stated that, "It is absolutely essential that all training stress: (1) Leadership, initiative, and aggressiveness. (2) Physical endurance. (3) Technical proficiency with weapons." The remaining four requirements dictated the conduct of inspections for equipment to be embarked as well as personnel inspections. Tactical inspections by the Commanding General could be expected any time a unit was in the field training, and finally, organizational commanders were directed to hold frequent inspections to ensure that all hands were equipped with and wearing the identification tags.

The 10th Marines guidance was to conduct normal training in artillery tactics, but with special emphasis on certain things that would be applicable to anticipated operations. As stated by the division training order, the artillerymen of the 10th Marines would.

>(1) Development of most efficient method of artillery support in atoll operations.
>
>(2) Conduct short-range overhead fire problems with infantry and tanks using forward observers to control and adjust fire.
>
>(3) Conduct battalion and regimental shoots. During these shoots opportunity will be given other units of the Division to familiarize themselves with the characteristics of overhead and close-supporting artillery fire.
>
>(4) Conduct field training to test control of fire from tank OP's.
>
>(5) All forward observers, whenever opportunity permits, will be ordered by this Headquarters to observe Naval Gunfire and will have practice in spotting.
>
>(6) Train one pack howitzer battery per battalion in the tactics and techniques of rubber boat landings.[3]

---

[3] Second Marine Division Training Order Number 33-43, Training Directive, Headquarters, Second Marine Division, Fleet Marine Force, December 30, 1943, In the Field.

One factor of training not given any emphasis for the artillerymen was the basic training of shooting their rifles or throwing grenades. Throughout the months of training, they were only trained in firing their howitzers. Those Marines who were in machinegun sections were given the opportunity to fire their machine guns only after pressing the request themselves. A factor of training that was given lots of emphasis was physical conditioning by way of hiking. Many a moan and groan were heard by the men of 5/10 as they often got a close and personal view of the Parker ranch. Major Hitt, the tall long legged battalion Executive Officer was especially feared for the hikes he led.[4]

One day a couple of the 5/10 Marines decided to do a little hiking of their own by way of a goat hunt. Lieutenant Buss and Corporal Claude Corbin received permission to go into one of the remote areas of the island where wild goats were known to exist. In one of the large canyons they hunted, Corbin spotted and was able to shoot a goat. After a very arduous effort to carry the goat back to camp to show off their prey, the Marines learned that even after getting rid of the goat they smelled like wild goats themselves. Showers and a change of clothes rectified the problem.[5]

In accordance with directives, training began for artillery units as they left the confines of Camp Tarawa and moved out into the training areas. The vast lava beds of Mauna Kea and Mauna Loa provided an excellent impact area for the howitzers to shoot into, but the Marines were amazed how quickly the lava rock wore on the soles of their boots. Wind was another element that the artillerymen had to deal with as it created a constant annoyance to the Marines as they trained.

The emphasis on combined training started the second week in January as artillery FO teams of 5/10 conducted a week-long school and training period to give mortar forward observer teams of the infantry some artillery training. Toward the latter part of January, the 10th Marines conducted an artillery demonstration for the rest of the division. According to Brigadier General M.L. Curry USMC, (Ret), this artillery demonstration was, "...intended to build in the infantry confidence in its artillery support;

---

[4] Faye O'Dell, Letter to author, Date unknown, Perry, Oklahoma.
[5] Claude E. Corbin, Letter to author, May 31, 1991, Bloomfield, Indiana.

also, to familiarize infantry with the ease of getting artillery support."[6]

Later in the training the division would conduct a live fire and maneuver training exercise as the tanks and infantry advanced under live overhead artillery fire with forward observers adjusting the fire on targets of opportunity. Much of the time however the artillery Marines of the 2d Division did not enjoy the action of live fire training as the "dry run" missions they fired seemed endless.

During February 8th to the 10th, Colonel Griffin had the regiment conduct a three-day field exercise based on a simulated landing. In concurrence with anticipated atoll operations, the artillery trained to refine its capability to support amphibious operations. Getting howitzers ashore and providing fast effective fire support was no small job.[7]

As they came out of the field the second week in February, the artillerymen looked ahead to another kind of training highlight. Major General Smith directed that a rodeo be conducted, and team competition would be held amongst the regiments. The Parker Ranch was happy to allow the Marines to use their facilities and they provided plenty of livestock for the events. There were plenty of eager young cowboys in the division willing to participate. The rodeo began with the traditional parade through the corral and then the competition began. There were two events in which only the Hawaiian Cowboys of the Parker Ranch competed; these were the pony express race and group roping exhibition. However, five events for the Marines included steer riding, wild cow milking, roping and bulldogging, mule racing, and bronco busting. PFC E. Wortman of Bozeman, Montana won the steer riding event for the 10th Marines. The winner of the wild cow milking contest also went to the artillery regiment as Corporal W. E. Lowry of Lyman, Nebraska won the event in 50 seconds. The third win for the artillery was by PFC A. Rodenberg of Luling, Texas and PFC G. Wade of Tucson, Arizona as they won the roping and bulldogging competition. PFC N. Wagner of Acamos, Co. took a second place in the mule race to get three more points for the artillery,

---

[6] Brigadier General M. Lamar Curry, USMC (Ret.), Telephone Interview, March, 1991, Lexington, Virginia.
[7] War Diary, Headquarters, Second Marine Division, Fleet Marine Force, March 1, 1944, In The Field.

bringing the regiments total to 18 and a first-place finish overall.[8]

One of the Marines in 5/10 who wanted to participate in the rodeo was PFC Eric Johnson. Although he had no rodeo experience, he was a tough Marine and figured he could hold on to any stupid cow for just eight seconds. As he sat down on the closely penned-in wild bull, Johnson firmly wrapped the rope around his hand to hold on as the bull was to be let out of the pen. When the gate opened the bull lunged out of the pen with Johnson on his back. As the bull did its first bucking jump, PFC Johnson found himself flying through the air and landing hard on the dusty ground. After they saw that he was okay, Johnsons buddies howled with laughter. They thought that seeing Eric get thrown like that was the highlight of the rodeo. The fact that Johnson won no points for his team did not matter a bit.[9]

Another interesting sidelight of the rodeo was the greased pig event. The Hawaiian cowboys caught and greased a wild boar for the event. Even though the ranch-hands cut off the tusks from the animal, when it was released from its cage it went crazy. Instead of running from the contestants who were there to catch it, the wild boar attacked the Marines and chased them all out of the corral.[10]

According to the division newspaper, Tarawa Boom De-Ay, at the barbecue that accompanied the rodeo the Marines of the 2d Division consumed 15,000 pounds of beef on the hoof, 420 pounds of cheese, 18,000 bottles of Coca Cola, and 22,500 bottles of beer. Even with all that beer consumed the division MP's had to lasso and hog tie only three Marines for their drunken behaviors.[11]

Along with several other reorganizational changes, the first day of March saw the 5th Battalion, 10th Marines redesignated as the 3rd Battalion, 10th Marines and vice versa. The Marines who used to be in N, O, & P batteries were now in G, H, & I batteries. In addition, one month

---

[8] Tarawa Boom De-Ay, Published By And For The Men Of The Second Marine Division, Number 7, Volume 1, February 18, 1944, Camp Tarawa, Hawaii.
[9] William J. Miller, Interview with author, September, 1992, Dubuque, Iowa.
[10] Tarawa Boom De-Ay, Published By And For The Men Of The Second Marine Division, Number 7, Volumne 1, February 18, 1944, Camp Tarawa, Hawaii.
[11] Tarawa Boom De-Ay, Published By And For The Men Of The Second Marine Division, Number 7, Volumne 1, February 18, 1944, Camp Tarawa, Hawaii.

later the new 5th Battalion was again given a new designation to become the 2d 155mm Artillery Battalion, Corps Artillery, V Amphibious Corps. This new corps artillery asset was attached to the 10th Marines so now the regiment had two 75mm pack howitzer battalions, 1st and 2d, two 105mm howitzer battalions, 3d and 4th, and the newly formed Corps Artillery 155mm battalion.[12]

On March 4th Major General Smith submitted a Report of Readiness of the 2d Division as of 29 February to the Commanding General of the V Amphibious Corps, Lieutenant General H. M. Smith. The first paragraph stated that Major General Smith thought his division was... "not in a state of complete readiness for amphibious operations involving a landing on hostile shores." The report went on to explain that the divisions lack of readiness was... "due to essential equipment shortages, incomplete training of replacements and insufficient jungle and amphibious training."

The training had been productive. Major General Smith reported that in the month of February training was intensive and progressive. As directed by the Division Training Order Number 33-43, heavy emphasis was put on combat practice firing, field exercises, and basic small unit training. Also, each infantry regiment had conducted a two-day air-ground exercise in conjunction with air and artillery support. One of the prime reasons for these exercises was to develop the technique and procedure required for efficient air-ground communication. By Smith's estimate, at the end of February the 2d Marines Division was only 65 percent ready for combat.[13]

Also published on the 4th of March was Division Training Memo # 42-44. This memo directed that an Aerial Observers (AO) School be conducted for the division from 6-25 March at the airfield at Hilo. Two officers would attend from the division headquarters, one officer from each infantry regiment, and eleven officers from the 10th Marines would

---

[12] David N. Buckner, Major, USMC, A Brief History Of The 10TH Marines, History and Museums Division, Headquarters, United States Marine Corps, 1981, Washington, D.C. p. 70.

[13] Report of Readiness as of 29 February, 1944, Headquarters, Second Marine Division, Fleet Marine Force, March 4, 1944, In the Field.

make up the class.[14]

The impetus for the AO training was the recent arrival of VMO-2. This Marine Observation Squadron was dedicated to supporting the 2d Marine Division. Nine officers and twenty-eight enlisted Marines, commanded by Major Bob Edmondson, arrived with 12 new OY-1 Stinson Sentinels. The small light airplanes were powered by 185 horsepower engines and built specifically with two seats to serve as platforms for aerial observation. Because of their small size and unique ability to get in and out of grass airfields, the aircraft were nicknamed "Grasshoppers."[15]

Lieutenant Al Pearson was one of the officers from 3/10 assigned to be trained as an aerial observer. In addition to training in the OY-1 aircraft, Pearson and the others flew in and trained from the heavier TBM torpedo bomber aircraft. The TBM's were aircraft carrier capable, something the smaller Grasshoppers were not. Plans called for using the TBM's to control naval gunfire and artillery missions until such time that adequate airfields could be secured ashore from which the OY-1's could operate. After their formal school ended, most of the men went back to their own units, but continued to practice their newly acquired skills on a regular basis. Lieutenant Pearson learned that the OY-1's would be transported to their next campaign aboard the aircraft carrier Midway after being put onboard by cranes. He learned soon after that he and other aerial observers would also go onboard the Midway for transport to wherever their next mission would be.[16]

Throughout the month of March, 3/10 continued to train in the huge lava beds created many years earlier by the now calm volcanos. Although the lava beds were not usable for a whole range of activities, the vast expanse of nothing served as a great training area to fire and adjust artillery. One of the disadvantages of training in the volcanic lava beds was the severe wear and tear on the men's boots. The abrasive surface

---

[14] Division Training Memorandum Number 42-44: Aerial Observer School, Headquarters, Second Marine Division, Fleet Marine Force, March 4, 1944, In the Field.
[15] Tarawa Boom De-Ay, Published By And For The Men Of The Second Marine Division, Number 11, Volume 1, March 17, 1944, Camp Tarawa, Hawaii.
[16] Albert Pearson, Interview with author, September, 1992, Dubuque, Iowa.

wore down the soles of the boots quickly.[17]

On the 28th of March, 2d Division Administrative Order Number 27 was published to provide exact guidance on the control of individual equipment. The second paragraph of that order read: 2. Enlisted personnel of this division will possess the below listed items of individual equipment, as appropriate to rank and duty:

1. Haversack, MCP, 1941.	14. Pole, shelter tent.
2. Knapsack, MCP, 1941.	15. Pins, tent, shelter.
3. Suspenders, MCP, 1941.	16. Net, mosquito,
4. Canteen, M1910.	17. Net, mosquito, head.
5. Can, meat, w/cover.	18. Pad, cotton.
6. Cup, canteen.	19. Protector, pad.
7. Cover, canteen.	20. Helmet
8. Knife, haversack.	21. Poncho, rubberized.
9. Spoon, haversack.	22. Mask, gas.
10. Fork, haversack.	23. Belt, cartridge, rifle.
11. Packet, 1st aid.	24. Basic weapon.[18]
12. Pouch, 1st aid.	
13. Tent, shelter half.	

On 2 April Division Training Memorandum Number 73-44 was issued announcing the inspection of the 10th Marines by the Commanding General. Unfortunately, that inspection never took place because, much to the dismay of Major General Smith and the Second Division, Major General Smith was being reassigned and therefore required to turn over the division.[19] The CG of the 2d Marine Division was held in the highest regard by his men. Major General Smith spent most of his stateside duty between Philadelphia, Washington, and Quantico. He also served expeditionary duty in the Caribbean and Central America. General Smith was awarded the Navy Cross for his heroic actions in Nicaragua, and received many other high laurels during his career. But the highlight of his

---

[17] Harold A. Lane, "Recollections of the 10th Marines," March, 1990, Santa Rosa, California, p. 7.
[18] Division Administrative Order Number 27: Control of Individual Equipment, Headquarters, Second Marine Division, Fleet Marine Force, 14 July 1944, In the Field.
[19] War Diary for April, 1944.

career was undoubtedly the time he spent as the commanding general of the 2d Marine Division.[20] He loved his men and they loved him. As one Marine in the 2d Division talked about his former CG, he let it be known that there were other general officers named Smith in the Corps at that time, but to them, "... there was only one Major General Smith."[21]

In his own words, General Smith, "... was pretty mad," about his orders to turn over command of the division. The major point of irritation was that General Smith had spoken with General Vandergrift just a week earlier at a meeting in Hawaii and the Commandant gave no indication that General Smith would not keep the division. But orders were orders and General Smith would execute his orders as directed.[22]

Training Memorandum Number 79-44 gave the specifics of the Change of Command parade which would take place at the Kamuela Ball Park at 0900 on April 10, 1944. The new division Commander would be Brigadier General Thomas E. Watson. Only two months earlier 'Gen Watson was the commander of expeditionary troops for Operation Catchpole, the assault and capture of the Eniwetok Atoll. Little could he have known at the time what a significant role Eniwetok would play in his future assignment.

Third Battalion, 10th Marines would represent the artillerymen at the parade. In addition to the band, there were five other battalions on line with a 16-man front at close interval. The uniform for the parade was to be khaki trousers, shirts, field scarfs, and caps, garrison service summer. Individual weapons were carried by all men in the parade. Because they were second from the left in formation, 3/10 entered the ball park through the South-East entrance at 0833 to assume position for the ceremony. Brigadier General M. A. Edson, famed for his exploits as a Marine Raider, was the Commander of Troops for the parade.[23]

---

[20] Interview with unidentified veteran of Second Marine Division at division reunion, February, 1992, Camp Lejeune, N.C.
[21] Mrs. Julian C. Smith, Interview with author, February, 1992, Camp Lejeune, North Carolina.
[22] Lieutenant General Julian C. Smith, USMC (Ret), Marine Corps Oral History Collection, Archives Branch, Marine Corps Research Center, Marine Corps University, Quantico, Virginia.
[23] Division Training Memorandum Number 79-44: Parade, Headquarters, Second Marine Division, Fleet Marine Force, April 9, 1944, In the Field.

Chapter 4

As always in war, there was much speculation and guessing about what the next objective would be. It was the middle of April when senior ranking officers of the division learned that a group of islands known as the Marianas would be their next target. The first stop at the Marianas would be a funny shaped island named Saipan. Although the dimensions of the island are given as approximately twelve miles long and six miles wide, there are two peninsulas that stick out from the east coast that create the appearance of a monkey wrench. Saipan is the second largest island of the Marianas archipelago, which was discovered by Magellan in 1521. The Spanish explorer named the islands for his queen, Marie Anne. Spain later sold the islands to Germany, but after World War II the League of Nations mandated Saipan to Japan, and Guam to the United States. As a result of its key location in the Pacific, the Japanese military used Saipan as a stopover and training area for its forces on their way to other locations to the south and the east.[1]

For security reasons, the target was not made known to the men of the division, so like everyone else the Marines of 3/10 continued their training and preparation without knowledge of their next objective. The first week in May saw the men making preparations for an upcoming large scale amphibious training exercise to be conducted at Maalaea Bay, Maui and Kahoolawe Island in Hawaiian waters. The third battalion would be in Tractor Group A along with the rest of the regiment. Between the 12th and 14th of May the artillery loaded their assigned ships at Hilo and Hapuna Bay. 3/10 was assigned to LST 71 which was manned by the Coast Guard instead of the Navy. It was not unusual for Marines to find themselves on a Coast Guard ship since during a time of war the Coast

---

[1] Henry I. Shaw, Jr., Bernard C. Nalty, and Edwin C. Turnbladh, History of U.S. Marine Corps Operations in WW II Central Pacific Drive, Volume III. (Washington: Historical Branch, G-3 Division, Headquarters, U.S. Marine Corps, 1966). p. 237.

Guard comes under the control of the Navy Department. In fact, some men claimed to prefer Coast Guard vessels because, according to Dodd Sellers, "The Coast Guard operated vessels always tried to give us decent food."[2]

Like every other LST (Landing Ship Tank), LST 71 had an LCT (Landing Craft Tank) loaded on her deck in order to transport the slower LCT across the ocean to the invasion sight. It was very common for the larger LST to carry the smaller LCTs and DUKW's (Amphibious Truck) from the embarkation point to the line of departure. The LCT's were craned onto the deck of the LST and set on huge blocks of wood, then secured to the deck of the LST with chains. The means of debarkation was simply to have the LST ballast down on one side causing the larger ship to list to that side. At a specified angle of list the LCT would be unshackled and gravity would cause the landing craft to slide off its blocks and into the water.

Three of the LCT's which were to be transported on an LST were specially modified to provide fire support to the Marine forces assaulting the beach. It was the idea of Rear Admiral Harry Hill to mount six 4.2 mortars, along with 2500 rounds of ammo, into each of the three LCT's. As long as there were LST's able to carry the smaller craft across the ocean, we were going to use them.[3]

The LST's were built more as an equipment transport than a troop transport. Normally the only men to ride the LST were the minimal required to support the equipment on board. However, during the short training exercise in the waters off Hawaii, all of 3/10 was aboard the LST. As a result of too many Marines and too little space, many men were pleased to find themselves sleeping on cots on the decks of the ship. This was much preferable to the hot cramped troop berthing areas below in the ship. Having the LCT onboard the LST actually created more room for 3/10. The large wooden blocks the LCT sat on were so big that many men slept under the LCT, shaded from the sun and rain. In addition, the

---

[2] Dodd Sellers, "As I Recall: Remembering 1941-1946," March 12, 1991, Tuscaloosa, Alabama. p. 33.
[3] Vice Admiral George Carrol Dyer, USN (Ret), The Amphibians Came To Conquer - The Story of Admiral Richard Kelly Turner, Volume II. (Washington: U.S. Government Printing Office, 1972). p. 893.

communication section of Headquarters & Service Battery, as well as a few other Marines from H&S Battery, were assigned to the LCT for its berthing and equipment storage area.[4]

The night of 15 April brought a severe storm to the Hawaiian Islands. Conditions on the seas were so bad that ships were not required to maintain any tactical formation, but do what they could to best weather the storm. However, there was nothing that LST 71 could do to prevent itself from being tossed around through the huge swells of the terrible storm that night. Back and forth the ship rocked. The smaller LCT was not subject to the pounding of the waves, but it was not safe from the wrath of the storm. As the larger ship shifted positions violently, the smaller craft would also shift within the confines of its restricting chains that secured it to the ship. With each successive roll of the LST, the strain on the chains securing the LCT became greater and greater until at 2:00 AM they finally ripped the welded bracket up from the ships deck. Two of the men sleeping under the LCT were Corporal Hugh Adams and PFC Delbert Porter. They were awakened as the smaller craft over them began to shift within its confines. Adams informed Porter that they might be wise to move. They scooted out from under the LCT, but a second before Porter was clear the chains broke and a large timber slammed into him breaking his arm.[5] The Marines inside the LCT felt themselves being launched into the water. Its engine room was flooded and so any chance of getting power to maneuver the craft was eliminated. The LCT was bobbing like a cork and in great danger. The danger was compounded by the fact that the Marines had no life jackets on in case they went into the water. Due to the serious consequences that were possible for the LCT, the LST violated normal procedures and turned on some lights and located the smaller craft in order to shoot a line to it. After successive lines of increasing size were pulled to the LCT by the 3/10 Marines, they secured the final line to the LCT and were in tow of the LST. For nearly 30 hours the H & S Battery Marines bobbed around in the LCT. Water cans and several cases of K-Rations were provided to them via the tow line.[6] Although their

---

[4] Hugh Adams, Letter to author, June 15, 1992, Joplin, Mo.
[5] Adams, Letter.
[6] Anthony B. Vouma, Letter to author, June 13, 1990, Encinitis, California.

situation was not a good one, the 3/10 Marines had to consider themselves fortunate as there were LCTs unintentionally launched that night that sank.[7]

Two of the LCT's that sank that night were 4.2 mortar gunships. According to the H&S 3/10 comm section, with a tarp over the LCT and the ramp up, it was muggy and kind of uncomfortable for the men inside the LCT. The 3/10 communicators asked the skipper of the craft to lower the ramp so that a breeze might get into the men. Although they were unhappy when he refused, they later sang a different tune after learning that those LCT's that launched with their ramp down quickly sank.[8] The loss of men and equipment that night was a serious problem by itself, however the event was to have much more severe consequences just days later as the ships and landing craft put into Pearl Harbor for repairs.

Even though the men on the LCT would have much rather been on the LST during the storm, those on the LST were having serious problems of their own. As a result of the severe beating that LST 71 had taken, she suffered a split in the hull below the double bottoms and was taking on water in the tank deck area. As soon as this was discovered the artillerymen formed a bucket brigade to assist in bailing the water out of the ship. In addition, mattresses were carried from the berthing areas and stuffed in certain areas to impede the flow of water. For a while the situation was not totally under control and instructions were given on how to abandon ship if it should be required. However, that was not to be the case as the sailors and Marines were able to control the intake of water and the ship made it to Pearl Harbor with the LCT in tow.[9]

LST 71 joined six other LSTs as she tied up at Pearl Harbors' West Loch for repairs. As a result of the storm, some of the ships had suffered major damage and would be replaced while others had suffered only minor damage and would be repaired at the West Loch. Senior officers determined that LST 71 was damaged too severely to be repaired in time,

---

[7] Henry I. Shaw, Jr., Bernard C. Nalty, and Edwin C. Turnbladh, History of U.S. Marine Corps Operations in WW II Central Pacific Drive, Volume III. (Washington: Historical Branch, G-3 Division, Headquarters, U.S. Marine Corps, 1966). p. 252.
[8] Vouma letter. 1990.
[9] Vouma letter. 1990.

so the men of 3/10 found themselves working continuously for 36 hours unloading their equipment and ammo in order to reload it onto another ship.[10]

On Sunday afternoon, May 21st, the 3/10 Marines were ashore in a temporary camp awaiting the arrival of a replacement ship. As the Marines lamented over their tough luck with the storm and its damage to their ship, they observed what real tough luck is. LST 3553 was the last LST tied up to 6 others in the harbor. Like the other ships it was loaded to the brim with its equipment in preparation for the coming invasion, and like many other ships it needed repairs. According to some accounts, a welder's torch created the sparks that fell to the tank deck where some gasoline drums were stored. As the residual gas ignited it caused the drums to explode which set off a chain reaction of tremendous explosions throughout the ship. Many men on the ship were killed instantly, others were severely hurt when they were blown off the ship. Others jumped for their lives to avoid the occurring catastrophe.[11] The 3/10 Marines found many men struggling ashore near their temporary camp and tried the best they could to help. One of the 3/10 corpsman was Pharmacist Mate Second Class Billy Stout, who had to treat many Marines for cuts they received from the razor-sharp grass after they arrived ashore.

Other accounts of the accident say that because two of the three LCT mortar gunboats were lost in the storm, the 4.2 mortar ammo was being offloaded from LST 3553 and a mishandled round was dropped and detonated causing the terrible chain of explosions. No matter what the cause of the accident, the amphibious armada could not accept any more loses of its ships.

LST 127 was the replacement ship designated to haul the equipment and some of the men of 3/10 to their next objective. The ship was loaded with howitzers, ammo, trucks and other equipment required for an artillery battalion to accomplish its mission in war. In addition, the LST had the new DUKWs aboard which would be used to assist in getting the howitzer ashore. The DUKWS, like LVTs, were eminently satisfactory

---

[10] Wilber J. Buss, Letter to author, May 18, 1990, Lake Elsinore, California.
[11] Charles R. Sheehan, Letter to "Follow Me," Offical Publication of the Second Marine Division Association, May-June, 1990. p. 12.

both in landing troops and transporting cargo. They carried cargo direct from ships to supply dumps, without the necessity for transfer either at the reef or at the beach, thereby greatly speeding supply of essential items to the front lines. During periods when heavy swells caused such unfavorable surf conditions at the beaches that LVTs and boats could only operate with considerable difficulty and danger, DUKWs rode the swells steadily and landed through the surf with apparent ease.

DUKWs had the basic disadvantages of the LVT slow speed, relatively small cargo capacity for size, and, like the LVT(2), they required lifting equipment for ready unloading; however they did not tear the roads to pieces and the driver had better all-around vision. They were found to be particularly useful in handling artillery from LSTs direct to emplacement positions and were considered to be an essential amphibious vehicle.[12]

---

[12] CTF-51 Operations Report, Marianas, 25 August, 1944. pp. 7-1,7-4.

Chapter 5

Although the whole battalion was aboard the LST for the short training exercise off Hawaii, for the transit to their next objective in the western Pacific most of the Marines in 3/10 were assigned to an APA. The APA was a troop transport and much faster than the amphibious ship. Left aboard the LST were about 275 men of the artillery battalion. This was the number that the ship was built to accommodate, and these men were required to care for the howitzers and other equipment on the LST. The LST and other slower ships were formed into Tractor Group A and departed Hawaii on May 25th for a designated staging area. Between the 25th and 29th the remaining Marines of the Second Division loaded aboard the ships of Transport Group A and on 30 May sailed for their next invasion staging area.[1]

After leaving Hawaii the Marines were told for the first time that their next objective would be Saipan. When this island and its adjacent islands were secured, they would provide airstrips close enough for U.S. long range bombers to strike mainland Japan and return to the airstrip.[2]

On the 8th Of June, Tractor Group A arrived at the designated staging area, Eniwetok. The next day Transport Group A also reached Eniwetok. As they arrived the Marines were transferred to their respective ships for the invasion of Saipan. At 1400 on June 9th, LST 127 and 3d Battalion, 10th Marines left Eniwetok and headed for Saipan. The trip from Eniwetok to Saipan was not a short one, but the Marines were more concerned about what lie ahead at Saipan than the crowded conditions of the ship they were on.

---

[1] War Diary, Headquarters, Second Marine Division, Fleet Marine Force, June 3, 1944, In the Field.
[2] Henry I. Shaw,Jr., Bernard C. Nalty, and Edwin C. Turnbladh, History of U.S. Marine Corps Operations in WW II Central Pacific Drive, Volume III. (Washington: Historical Branch, G-3 Division, Headquarters, U.S. Marine Corps, 1966). p. 236.

The assault and capture of Saipan was not the sole responsibility of the 2d Marine Division. Also assaulting the heavily defended island would be the 4th Marine Division. The Army's 27th Division was the third major unit of the V Amphibious Corps, which was commanded by Lieutenant General H. M. Smith. The Marines and soldiers of Gen Smiths' assault force were designated: Northern Troops and Landing Force. The invasion of the Marianas was given the code name of Forager; it was officially Operation Plan 3-44 and was to be executed accordingly:

> Brief of Plan: Northern Troops and Landing Force, in conjunction with Northern Attack Force, will, on D-day, land, seize, occupy and defend SAIPAN ISLAND, and then will be prepared for further operations to seize, occupy and defend TINIAN ISLAND, in order to obtain the use of those islands and to destroy the enemy thereon. 2d Marine Division (Reinforced), at H-Hour on D-day, lands on Beaches RED and GREEN, seize objective O-1 in assigned zone of action; then, on Division order, advance rapidly and seize MT TAPOTCHAU - MT TIP PALE and that part of SAIPAN ISLAND in its assigned zone of action; protect the left (North) flank of the Northern Landing Force. Be prepared for further operations on order. 4th Marine Division (reinforced), at H-hour on D-day, land on Beaches Blue and Yellow, seize objective O-1 in assigned zone of action; then, on Division order, advance rapidly and seize ASLITO Airfield and that part of SAIPAN ISLAND in its assigned zone of action. Be prepared for further operations on order.[3]

---

[3] NTLF OP-PLAN 3-44, Forager, 1 May, 1944.

Chapter 6

On the evening of 14 June, the amphibious armada arrived off the western coast of Saipan. The artillerymen could see naval gunfire ships off in the distance prepping the island. Tons and tons of high explosive ordnance was fired onto the beaches and further inland of the assault beaches. Previous experience taught Naval forces that a well dug-in enemy was very hard to root out.

In the very early morning hours of June 15 the Marines awoke to see to last minute preparations prior to the assault. The traditional invasion breakfast of steak and eggs was served. This meal was commonly referred to by many of the Marines as "... the last supper."[1]

One of the Marines in 3/10 who clearly got off on the wrong foot while preparing to go ashore that early morning was Corporal Thomas Kane of George Battery. As the NCO in charge of the battery .50 caliber machinegun section, it was his responsibility to get the machineguns ashore properly. Going into one of the ships dark storage holes, where the .50 calibers were kept, Kane started to lift a machinegun box when a large heavy reel of communication wire fell on his right foot and smashed his big toe. The pain was severe enough that Kane went to see a corpsman. The corpsman drilled through the toenail to allow the blood to escape and then told Kane that he would most likely lose the nail. To this Kane gave a nonchalant nod of acknowledgment; but when the corpsman told the Marine corporal that he wouldn't have to go ashore, Kane's response was, "You have to be kidding..." There was no way he was staying behind.[2]

The first action of June 15th was a diversionary demonstration off Saipan's' northern coast conducted by Combat Team 2 (CT 2). Ships arrived in the northern waters at 0600 and launched the fake assault. Meanwhile the primary assault was beginning on the southern one-third of

---

[1] Hugh Adams, Letter to author, June 15, 1992, Joplin, Missouri.
[2] Thomas Kane, Letter to author, August 27, 1992, West Mifflin, Pennsylvania.

Saipan's western coast. The invasion beaches for the two Marine Divisions would be split by the town of Charan Kanoa. For the 2d Marine Division, Combat Teams 6 and 8 assaulted the shores in the face of heavy fire, but this was nothing new to them. After overcoming a certain amount of confusion as a result of landings on wrong beaches, the Marines pressed inward against heavy Japanese mortar and artillery fire. Japanese resistance was very intense and landing forces had great difficulty reaching their assigned objectives. It was not until 1500 that the battalion landing teams of the two regimental combat teams had gained enough of a beachhead that Brigadier General Mike Edson, assistant division commander still offshore in his command & control vessel, reported that CT 6 and CT 8 were set-up shore. As a result of this, CT 2 was ordered to send in its landing teams in columns.[3]

To strengthen his combat power onshore, General Watson ordered ashore the 1st and 2nd Battalions of the 10th Marines with their Pack 75mm Howitzers. A large beachhead was not established, but according to Lieutenant Colonel George Shell, CO of the 2nd Battalion, "...Higher authority felt it important to have the pack howitzers ashore to back up the regiments the night of D-day"[4] (For Lieutenant Colonel Shell the Saipan campaign would end the next day while he was standing by his jeep talking on the radio and a Japanese artillery round impacted close to him and wounded him badly enough to be evacuated.) By 1510 the 2nd Tank Battalion was successfully landing. It was also at this time that General Edson landed and established division control ashore. By 1730 Colonel Griffin landed over Red Beach 2 with the command element of the 10th Marines and established his command post near the division HQ. As the situation ashore was assessed, it was obvious that there was not enough room ashore to bring in the 3rd and 4th artillery battalions with their 105's.

It had been a hard-fought battle to establish what little beachhead the Marines owned, and by 1800 of the first day, the 2nd Division casualties were 238 KIA, 1022 WIA, and 315 MIA. However, the men knew the worst may still lie ahead of them as darkness approached. As

---

[3] War Diary, Headquarters, Second Marine Division, Fleet Marine Force, September 7, 1944, In the Field.
[4] Brigadier General George Shell, USMC (Ret), Letter to author, February 9, 1992, Lexington, Virginia.

they consolidated their positions and replenished their ammunition, observation aircraft noticed and reported a formation of Japanese tanks to the north. Throughout the night the Marines repelled Japanese counterattacks. Combined tank and infantry attacks on occasion penetrated the Marines lines, but their defense was never broken. A coordinated effort by the 2nd Division broke up and destroyed the Japanese attack and left burning Japanese tank hulls around the battlefield. At 0700 on the 16th the 2nd Marine Division continued its attack inland.[5]

---

[5] War Diary, September 7, 1944.

Chapter 7

By early afternoon, Green Beach 3 was secured with a large enough beachhead that the 3rd and 4th Battalions of the 10th Marines were able to land with their 105mm howitzers. These larger howitzers were landed in DUKWs (Amphibious Trucks) which used a built-in A-frame hoist to lift the 5000-pound howitzer out of the DUKW and onto the ground. Although in some cases DUKWs were used to transport the howitzers, the prime mover of the weapon was the FWD truck which landed in a separate landing craft.

The first members of 3/10 to go ashore were the battalion commander and his advance party. Traveling to the beach in an LVT (Landing Vehicle-Tracked), they were met at Green Beach 3 by the regimental operations officer, and former battalion commander, Major Hiett. The initial position that the artillery battalion would occupy was just northwest of Charan Kanoa. On the map this location was in the sector of TA 147 Dog. The batteries of 3/10 came ashore and quickly occupied their initial firing positions, for although the beach was secure enough to get ashore, there wasn't much room to go inland. 3/10's Marines, like the other artillerymen, laid in their guns amidst incoming Japanese artillery and mortar fire.[1] As incoming Japanese artillery hammered their positions, some Marines found themselves taking cover in nearby holes the Japanese had dug to repulse the Marines attack. Other holes were dug close to locations where the men would work. It did not take long for those Marines who occupied holes full of water to realize that being wet was a small price to pay in order to have some protection from the incoming enemy fire.[2]

The entire battalion position was located from the edge of the beach to the coast road just a few hundred yards inland. The position was

---

[1] Multiple interviews at reunions of Third Battalion, Tenth Marines, 1990 and 1992, Dubuque, Iowa.
[2] Rod Sandburg, "Battery "O" 5th Bn.," Date unknown, Bixby, Oklahoma. p. 2.

not a good one as it was located near the bottom of the sugar mill smoke-stack, just north of the town of Charan Kanoa. This provided an ideal reference point for the Japanese to use in order to call in artillery fire on the units nearby, specifically the 10th Marines. The artillery men's suspicions were later confirmed when a Japanese spotter was located in the old smoke stack where he had been adjusting fire onto the batteries of the 10th Marines.[3]

PFC Fayette Ellis was very happy to get ashore as Japanese rounds fell all around his landing craft as they came ashore. Ellis worked in the G Battery Fire Direction Center (FDC), which was set up by digging an 18inch pit in the sand and putting up an 8-man pyramidal tent over the top. Lanterns were used to provide light to work in the tent, and the tent flaps were kept tightly closed at night to prevent light from escaping and giving the Japanese a good target at which to shoot.[4]

Another problem with 3/10's initial position was that the 2d Division was unable to get its logistics build-up off the beach as fast as it was being brought in. The Navy was in a big hurry to get its ships unloaded and far out to sea in order to be in a better position to react to the Japanese fleet if the need arose. For this reason, the landing craft dumped their loads on the beach and headed back to sea. By late afternoon of the 17th over 33,000 tons had been offloaded to support the landing force. And much of the logistic support piling up was ammunition.[5]

The road that went north along the coast out of Charan Kanoa passed through the 3/10 position. It was at this location that the road was very straight and level and therefore functional as a runway. It was this stretch of road on which VMO-2 would land some of its observation aircraft from the carrier. These aircraft would be used extensively to adjust the artillery of the 10th Marines. Until the Grasshoppers could come ashore, Lieutenant Pearson and the other aerial observers would call for and adjust fire from the Navy's TBMs off the aircraft carriers. According

---

[3] Major Carl Hoffman, USMC, Saipan: The Beginning of the End, Historical Division, Headquarters, United States Marine Corps, 1950, Washington, D.C. p. 38.
[4] Fayette Ellis, Letter to author, February 18, 1992, Irving, Texas.
[5] Henry I. Shaw, Jr., Bernard C. Nalty, and Edwin C. Turnbladh, History of U.S. Marine Corps Operations in WW II Central Pacific Drive, Volume III. (Washington: Historical Branch, G-3 Division, Headquarters, U.S. Marine Corps, 1966). p. 291.

to Pearson, each time the TBMs took off from the carrier to go on an observation mission they would have a load of bombs onboard as well and conduct a bombing run on a likely target first. In addition to being a bomber with good visibility to do aerial observing, the TBMs also had an internal machinegun that could be used for air-to-air combat if necessary. Although the aerial observers received training on the use of the TBM machinegun, the American forces had such air supremacy that there was never an occasion to use it.[6]

Even though there were problems with the position that 3/10 was in, that was their position and they would have to make the best of it. In order to do this the Marines had to dig in to protect themselves from incoming Japanese fire while they provided artillery support for the other Marines ashore. As quickly as the firing batteries were layed, they conducted registrations with forward observers controlling the fire. The evening of 16 June, 3rd Battalion was assigned the mission of reinforcing the fires of the 1st Battalion which was in direct support of Combat Team 6.[7] In order to do this 3/10 established communications with 1/10's fire direction center at 1940.

As much as possible, the artillery used the ever-reliable wire landline to talk, but when the situation demanded radio communication the SCR 300 or SCR 610 was used. While these were both good radios, they were only good for line-of-sight communications. It was not uncommon for the radio operators to have to position themselves on a piece of high ground in order to talk to the battery or battalion. Only functioning with line-of-sight capability also required extensive use of relay positions. The evening of the 16th, the battalion learned that it had suffered its first casualties. Lieutenant Edward Burleigh, Sergeant Fred Polschuk, and Corporal Cornelius Muellner had gone ashore as part of the battalion reconnaissance party. They were killed by Japanese artillery fire shortly after arriving ashore with the reconnaissance party and survey team. Sergeant Kenneth Hill was severely wounded and had to be evacuated.[8]

Throughout the evening of June 16th, the Marines took incoming

---

[6] Albert Pearson, Interview with author, September 11, 1992, Dubuque, Iowa.
[7] Special Action Report, Headquarters, Tenth Marines, Second Marine Division, Fleet Marine Force, In the Field, 22 July 1944.
[8] Ibid.

artillery and mortar fire as they had during the day. Although the caliber of incoming Japanese rounds was probably varied, one Marine in 3/10 described the incoming rounds as, "...what I would think a 55 gallons oil drum would sound like if it was tumbling end over end at a high rate of speed coming in my direction."[9] As the darkness of the night surrounded the artillerymen, they would also have to increase their state of alertness and local security to guard against Japanese infiltrators. Even though the artillery was behind friendly lines of protection the Japanese were known to hide, play dead, or simply sneak through gaps in friendly lines in order to get at rear echelons of the Marine forces. Knowing this all units were on the alert and established local security to protect their area. The battery commander of How Battery, 3/10 had his security out that first night ashore. But Captain Harold Nelson was concerned about his sentries being very nervous and shooting at shadows, so he admonished them that if he heard any shots fired, he had better see a dead Japanese to go with it.[10]

PFC Ray Sarazin saw a figure moving stealthily through the night. Although it was dark, the short man in a Japanese uniform was clearly visible to Sarazin. Just as he learned in his Marine Corps training, the young Marine aligned the Japanese in his sights and squeezed the trigger of his weapon. As soon as Captain Nelson heard the shot crack through the night, the battery commander was heading toward the foxhole the shot had come from. As he came close enough to see PFC Sarazin the battery commander demanded to know where the dead Japanese was. "Right there, Captain," was Sarazin's reply as he pointed to the dead figure on the ground close to where the captain stood. It didn't take long for the word to get around.[11]

Unfortunately, not all the friendly fire that evening was aimed at infiltrating Japanese. On the G Battery perimeter PFC Wilbur Croxton was manning a machinegun position. As he felt the need to relieve himself, Croxton crawled a short distance away from the machinegun. In order to maintain a low silhouette, he only got up on his knees to urinate. Suddenly Croxton was felled by a shot from an unknown location. Immediate

---

[9] Wilbur Buss, Letter to author, May 18, 1990, Lake Elsinore, California.
[10] Rod Sandberg, "Battery "O" 5th Bn. (Sic), Date unknown, Bixby, Oklahoma, p. 4.
[11] Ray Sarazin, Letter to author, March 4, 1991, Esko, Minnesota.

suspicions were that a Japanese sniper was in range of the G Battery location. Croxton was badly wounded and in need of medical attention so the battery executive officer, Lieutenant Charlie Fallon, called for his corpsman to respond. Pharmacist Mate Second Class Billy Stout and three Marines crawled toward the battery perimeter and Croxton's location with a stretcher. It was a difficult crawl as they attempted to hurry to assist Croxton, for they had to stay low in order not to become victims of the sniper themselves. As Stout and the others arrived at Croxtons position they began to treat the wounded Marine. In the process of doing so, they received word that it had not been a Japanese sniper after all. The shot that wounded Croxton was fired by a nervous Seabee from the adjacent unit. As the wounded Marine was being evacuated and the confusion was getting sorted out, the man who shot Croxton explained that he shot without checking because he knew his target had to be a Japanese since he was so short.[12]

About 0645 on 17 June, 3/10 received orders that it was to reinforce the fires of 2/10, which was in direct support of Combat Team 8. So that day the 3rd Battalion artillerymen responded to calls from the 2nd Battalion as it fired in support of CT 8's drive inland. CT 8 was attempting to take control of the land east of Charan Kanoa and around Lake Susupe.[13] Throughout the day there was more than just artillery work going on inside the 3/10 position. The long straight stretch of road through the 3/10 position was called The Charan Kanoa Airstrip. By early evening of the 17th the small airstrip was ready and the first artillery spotting plane of VMO-2 landed at 1815 from the Navy carrier which transported it to Saipan. Although the OY-1's launched from the carrier, they were not fitted with a landing hook to catch the carriers arresting cables, so after taking off there was no returning to the carrier. The primary field they would operate out of would be the captured Aslito Airfield. Although Aslito was a much larger airstrip, there were many occasions when use of the smaller strip would be advantageous. One of the advantages was to make direct liaison with the artillery

---

[12] William Stout, Interview with author, September 11, 1992, Dubuque, Iowa.
[13] Special Action Report, Tenth Marines.

unit the aircraft would be spotting for.[14]

The evening of June 17th, as one of the small OY-1 aircraft, or grasshopper as it was referred to, attempted to take off it suddenly went down and crashed into one of the ammunition dumps was established just off the beach near the 3/10 position. Marines from H Battery were closest to the scene and ran quickly to assist. To their anguish they were only able to pull the observer from the burning aircraft. The pilot, 2nd Lieutenant Richard Orrok, was pinned in the plane and the spreading flames engulfed him quickly. As the flames spread, it was obvious that the ammunition would soon explode.[15]

In order to tell the regimental commander what had happened and warn of the impending danger, Major Crouch (Call sign - Romance) instructed his radio operator, PFC Dodd Sellers, to send the following transmission to Colonel Griffin (Call sign - Princess) at regimental headquarters.

> "Princess, Romance - Plane crashed in ammunition dump. Plane in flames. Ammunition expected to go momentarily. Warn all personnel in vicinity. BN6"[16]

As the fire burned dangerously, Lieutenant Buss went south on the beach in hopes of finding a water pump that could be brought to the 3/10 position to put out the raging fire. By the time he gave up his search for a pump it had turned dark, and no one was allowed to travel anywhere after dark. So, the 3/10 communication officer was forced to spend the night on the beach where the sand crabs kept him awake all night.[17] Lieutenant Buss could have stayed in the position as there was very little anyone could do except stay low and out of danger from the exploding ammunition until it expended itself. Several hours later a bulldozer was brought up from the beach by shore party and the fires were able to be contained. Also on the 17th, Lt Gen. Smith moved his Corps headquarters

---

[14] Albert Pearson, Interview with author, September 12, 1992, Dubuque, Iowa.
[15] Multiple interviews at reunions of Third Battalion, Tenth Marines, 1990 and 1992, Dubuque, Iowa.
[16] Dodd Sellers, Letter to author enclosing copies of original message of 1944, March 17, 1991, Tuscaloosa, Alabama.
[17] Wilber Buss, Letter to author, May 18, 1990, Lake Elsinore, California.

ashore near Charan Kanoa.[18]

Elsewhere in the regiment, the 17th proved to be a terrible day for the artillery of the 10th Marines as heavy Japanese artillery fire pounded the 2nd and 4th Battalions and inflicted heavy losses in both men and material. To their good fortune the men of 3rd Battalion did not sustain the amount of casualties and equipment damage that some of the other units did, even though all the units on or near the beachhead were constantly susceptible to Japanese artillery, mortar, and small arms fire.[19]

On the 18th the 4th Marine Division ran into some strong Japanese resistance. As a result of this, the 105mm howitzers of 3/10 and 4/10 were tasked to provide reinforcing fires for the 14th Marines, the artillery regiment of the 4th Division. After release from control of the 14th Marines, 3/10 went into general support of the 2nd Division.[20]

Throughout initial operations ashore artillery procedures ran smoothly. Much of the credit for this belonged to good communications between the artillery forward observers and the infantry and the artillery battalion. The main factor in the good communications was the closeness of the infantry to the artillery which allowed the SCR-300 and SCR-610 line of sight radios to operate clearly. Later as the maneuvering infantry got farther away and beyond intervening hills, it was necessary to establish relay stations manned by 3/10 communicators to pass along the call for fire to the FDC from the forward observers with the rifle battalions.[21]

---

[18] Henry I. Shaw, Jr., Bernard C. Nalty, and Edwin C. Turnbladh, History of U.S. Marine Corps Operations in WW II Central Pacific Drive, Volume III. (Washington: Historical Branch, G-3 Division, Headquarters, U.S. Marine Corps, 1966). p. 291.
[19] Special Action Report, 10th Marines.
[20] Special Action Report, 10th Marines.
[21] Wade Hitt, Interview with author, March, 1990, Fredericksburg, Virginia.

Chapter 8

All during the 19th, and until the evening of the 20th, 3/10 was again called on to fire reinforcing support of the 14th Marines.[1] During the night of 21 June, a Japanese infiltrator was able to get through the Marines' defensive perimeter and blow up another ammunition dump established between the positions of the 2nd and 3rd Artillery Battalions. A sentry from 2/10 saw the Japanese, but was too late to stop him. As the fire and explosion burned, Captain Carl A. Nielson, the 2nd Battalion logistics officer, led 12 Marines from the 2nd Battalion into the burning ammunition dump in an attempt to control the fire. However, a sudden explosion killed all but the captain and one other Marine. Shortly thereafter the executive officer of 3/10, Major Wade Hitt, led several men from 3/10 into the burning danger area to attempt to rescue any survivors of the fire and explosion. Corporal Charles Klotz was a member of the rescue team that went in with Major Hitt. According to Klotz, the attempted rescue almost became another tragedy when a member of the rescue party became unnerved as they entered the extremely dangerous burning ammunition dump. For some reason the Marine started screaming and wildly shooting the weapon he was carrying. Fortunately, Major Hitt was close enough to quickly grab the crazed man and take away his weapon. He was sent to the hospital for treatment.[2]

By the 22nd, the infantry regiments had completed their turning movement and the southern part of the island was secured. As a result, the Marines would begin their drive northward. At 0600 on 22 June, 3/10 joined seventeen other U.S. artillery battalions in conducting a 10-minute prep to kick off the NTLF offensive north toward Marpi Point, the northernmost part of the island. Later in the day 3/10 was given orders to

---

[1] Special Action Report, Headquarters, Tenth Marines, Second Marine Division, Fleet Marine Force, In the Field, 22 July 1944.
[2] Charles Klotz, Interview with author, June, 1989, Roaring Spring, Pennsylvania.

conduct a reconnaissance of map sector TA 172 for the purpose of selecting a new position to occupy. This new position would get the battalion off the beach and put them inland at the southwest corner of Mt Tapotchau, the high, densely-covered mountain at the center of Saipan. Positions for the batteries were selected and prepared, survey was also put in, but the order to move had not yet arrived.[3]

The night of 23 June, disaster struck the 10th Marines regimental headquarters as Japanese artillery hammered the command post and fire direction center. Lieutenant Colonel Forsyth, regimental executive officer, and Sergeant Major Baker, regimental sergeant major, were both killed. The regimental operations officer, former commanding officer of 3/10, Major Hiett, was seriously injured and was evacuated. As a result of these deaths and injuries some personnel changes were made. Third battalion lost its executive officer, Major Hitt, when he was assigned as the regimental operations officer. During the transition of personnel and because much of the regimental fire direction center was seriously damaged, Colonel Griffin shifted his command post to 1/10 for a couple days, but the commanding officer of 1/10, Colonel Rixey, became the new full time regimental executive officer.[4]

It was the 24th of June before the Japanese defending the area around Mt Tipo Pale, and southwest of Mt Tapotchau, were finally pushed northward, allowing the 2nd Division to declare the area secured. As a result of this, the order for 3/10 to finally displace to its new position at the bottom of Mt Tapotchau came about 1025 on 25 June. They displaced one battery at a time until the whole battalion was in the new position and ready to fire by 1700. Unlike the flat, sandy, beach they had previously occupied, this location was green rolling terrain at an altitude of about 150 feet above sea level. Most of the men could look behind their position and see the batteries of the 155 battalion. To the west they could see the position they just came from where stacks of supplies were accumulating. On the second day beach activity stopped and the Marines observed the ships leaving the coast of Saipan. First

---

[3] Special Action Report, Tenth Marines.
[4] War Diary, Headquarters, Second Marine Division, Fleet Marine Force, September 7, 1944, In the Field.

Sergeant Allen Ball of G Battery remembers the ships departure as, "...leaving us with an awful empty feeling."[5] Perhaps for some of the men the bad memories of Guadalcanal still lingered. The reason for the Navy's departure was the intelligence report that the Japanese fleet was on its way to the Marianas. This move would have a disastrous effect on the Japanese fleet as the American Navy fought the Marianas Turkey Shoot and shot down 476 Japanese aircraft and sunk 23 Japanese ships.[6]

One of the unwelcomed similarities between the second and first positions of 3/10 was the Japanese shelling. At least the second position offered better ground in which to dig protective fox holes. Corporal Leo Mickalowski of George Battery dug a good hole for himself. Then he went to the trouble of placing some heavy logs over it in order to provide overhead protection. That night as Mickalowski lay resting in his hole two terrifying things happened almost simultaneously. The Japanese started shelling the 3/10 area, and suddenly Mick felt something crawl quickly across his face. So startled was the corporal that he jumped out of the foxhole onto the open ground. And even though the area continued to receive incoming Japanese artillery for a short while longer, Mickalowski preferred taking his chances against the enemy artillery rather than go back down in that dark hole with whatever was down there.[7]

At the second position, some of the men caught wind of a rumor that local natives claimed a nearby cemetery contained the remains of Amelia Earhart. Although there was a great deal of skepticism about the native rumor, curiosity got the best of some. One day during a lull in the firing Corporal Claude Corbin was asked to accompany one of the H&S Battery officers to go and check out the cemetery just to see if there was any validity to the story. On the way rumor was forced to give way to reality as Corbin spotted a wounded Japanese who tried to hide in a small hut. The unarmed Japanese was captured and taken back to the battalion area where he was treated for his wound by Dr. Zinberg, the battalion surgeon. Whether or not the captured Japanese was afraid of being

---

[5] Allen Ball, Letter to author, March 4, 1992, Bakersfield, California.
[6] Henry I. Shaw, Jr., Bernard C. Nalty, and Edwin C. Turnbladh, History of U.S. Marine Corps Operations in WW II Central Pacific Drive, Volume III. (Washington: Historical Branch, G-3 Division, Headquarters, U.S. Marine Corps, 1966), p. 298.
[7] Leo Mickalowski, Interview with author, September 11, 1992, Dubuque, Iowa.

interrogated was unknown, for shortly after the doctor dressed his wound, he made a break to escape but was shot dead by Marines in the area. No one ever verified the Amelia Earhart rumor.[8]

At the second position, 3/10 was assigned the mission of direct support of Combat Team 8.[9] Shortly after receiving the mission, the battalion was called on to provide heavy artillery fire onto the upper slopes of Mt Tapotchau where LT 1/29, still attached to CT 8, was making the steep ascent to the top. With LT 1/29 was a 3/10 artillery forward observer (FO) team from H battery consisting of Lieutenant Hal Lane, Sergeant Richard Matthews, Corporal Donald Irwin, and PFC Thomas Moretti. Although they called in much artillery support on the way up the mountain, during the close attack phase to take the mountain top the FO team would do its part as assault Marines along with the rest of the battalion. Lane and the other three men were handed some grenades from a box carried by a bearded sergeant with a toothpick hanging from his mouth. As the four artillerymen took some grenades, the sergeant grinned and said to Lieutenant Lane and his FO. team, "You guys are lucky. We might get into some hand-to-hand combat. This here is a real war."[10]

As it turned out the Marines were able to secure the unoccupied top of the mountain, but soon found themselves in serious combat repelling the Japanese attacks to retake the key high ground. The Marines were able to successfully hold the mountain and then occupied the right side as the division pushed northward. The steep slopes of the mountain ravines made the going slow, but the Marines maintained steady pressure and pushed the Japanese back.[11]

During the push north, as the Marines of 3/10 occupied the battalion observation post (OP) with the maneuvering infantry, they fired many artillery missions in support of the maneuvering infantry. In some instances, however, the Japanese were so close that company mortars were

---

[8] Claude Corbin, Letter to author, May 31, 1991, Bloomfield, Indiana.
[9] Special Action Report, Tenth Marines.
[10] Harold A. Lane, "Recollections of the 10th Marines," March, 1990, Santa Rosa, California, p. 10.
[11] Captain James Stockman, USMC, "The Taking of Mt. Tapotchau," Marine Corps Gazette, July, 1946, pp. 15-20.

the largest caliber weapon than could be used.[12]

In the sky over Mt Tapotchau was a TBM aircraft on observation duty. Lieutenant Al Pearson was the observer and the plane was piloted by a Navy Lieutenant named Lopez. As they watched the battle unfolding below them, they saw many occasions when the fighting was at very close quarters between American and Japanese forces. As Marine tanks were working their way up the mountain to provide some heavy direct fire support, Pearson and Lopez noticed several Japanese soldiers come out of the bushes and jump on top of one of the tanks. Lieutenant Lopez immediately put the TBM into a dive toward the tank. Not knowing how vulnerable the tank may be to the attacking enemy, Lopez flew his aircraft within a few yards of the tank and successfully scattered the Japanese off the tank. Climbing out of the dive and then looking back toward the tank, the pilot and aerial observer noticed the Japanese again positioning themselves to get on the Marine tank. Lopez again put his aircraft into a dive to chase off the aggressive attackers. However, this time as the TBM buzzed the tank to scatter the Japanese the element of surprise was gone and the aircraft was fired upon by the Japanese. The aircraft was hit but the extent of the damage was unknown. Immediately the pilot turned the aircraft toward the carrier where a safe landing was made. It was fortunate for Lieutenants Lopez and Pearson that the carrier was not a lot farther away because as Lopez brought the plane to a stop on the flightdeck the last drops of remaining gasoline trickled from the Japanese bullet holes in the planes gas tanks.[13] Also working with CT 8 to take Mt. Tapotchau was a 3/10 forward observer team attached to LT 2/8. Lieutenant Walter Bakula, PFC James Tucker, Corporal Martin Ener, and PFC Max Timmons were calling in artillery fire on the Japanese from 3/10 howitzers at the base of the mountain. However, 2/8 was taking a pounding from Japanese artillery located to the north. In an effort to observe where the Japanese fire was coming from, the FO team moved dangerously close to the edge of the cliff that overlooked the terrain to the north. It was just then that another volley of Japanese artillery struck and knocked Ener off the

---

[12] Lane, Recollections, p. 11.
[13] Albert Pearson, Interview with author, September 12, 1992, Dubuque, Iowa.

cliff to his death 200 feet below.[14]

Although the Marines normally ate K-rations, it was on Mt Tapotchau one day that PFC Moretti was able to acquire from the Army, for the FO team, what were referred to as 10 in 1 rations. After eating the rations, the whole team got sick. According to Sergeant Matthews, the rations were very acceptable except that a serving of pork sausage made him so sick that he would never eat pork sausage again.[15]

3/10 remained in direct support of CT 8 until 4 July. By that time the infantry was approaching the 11,000 meters range of the 105mm howitzers. In order to be in position to provide support as American forces moved forward in a Northeasterly direction, at 1520 on 4 July, 3/10 received orders to displace.[16] The new firing position was just a little inland from the small peninsula of Mutcho Point, on Saipan's west coast. This position was a little east-northeast of the city of Garapan. As usual, the batteries displaced one by one to ensure that at least 2 of the batteries were able to support at all times. Occupation and registration were completed for the battalion by 1905. The battalion's mission was now general support of the entire division. It would receive instructions on what targets to fire on from the division headquarters. However, 3/10 was not called on to provide much artillery fire while at this position. To make matters worse, most of the Marines were hearing scuttlebutt that the Japanese were pretty much defeated and for the most part it would be a lot of mopping up operations. Consequently, there was some idle time at their new position near the war-torn city of Garapan.

The city of Garapan had been staunchly defended by the Japanese and as a result took a terrible beating from American naval gunfire, air and artillery to soften it up for the attacking Marines. Lieutenant Pearson vividly remembers the tremendous amount of firepower brought to bear on Garapan that day. He recounts that, "I fired naval gunfire for 8 hours at Garapan from a TBM."[17] Even though much of Garapan lay in rubble, the position that 3/10 occupied was not that bad. Ironically, they established their artillery position near what had been the Garapan Naval Depot. There

---

[14] James Tucker, Interview with author, September 11, 1992, Dubuque, Iowa.
[15] Richard Matthews, Letter to author, May 11, 1990, Fresno, California.
[16] Special Action Report, 10th Marines.
[17] Pearson interview.

were various weapons of different calibers throughout the area. An accurate count of these weapons showed that three 5" coast defense guns, one 140mm coast defense gun, thirty-two 120mm dual purpose guns, and six 200mm mortars were lying about the area.[18] It was obvious to the Marines that they were fortunate that the Japanese did not have sufficient time or materials to install the big guns.

George Battery established its position near several concrete gun emplacements still intact. James Tucker recalls that the battery used one of the concrete structures as the location for the battery CP. The circular structures were about 10 feet in diameter and 6 feet high. Also near the position were many concrete pillars that had supported buildings on top of them. But these buildings were not concrete and therefore did not survive the bombardment, leaving only charred rubble.[19]

In that same area, some Marines of 3/10 found an abandoned cache of Japanese rice wine, or Saki as it is more commonly known. That evening there were a few men who felt the power of the Saki they drank. There were some other Marines who did not have the good fortune to find some liquid spirits to indulge in, but used a little home remedy to satisfy their thirst. From the mess tent one of them acquired several pounds of raisins while several others went looking for the battalion aid station. As a couple of the Marines distracted the corpsman, another was able to quickly steal a few bottles of alcohol from the medicine chest. After mixing the raisins and alcohol together there was nothing to do but wait as long as they could for the mixture to ripen. By the next evening the cleanest shirt they could find served as the strainer to pour the mixture through. While it was not the best stuff they ever tasted, all agreed that their field-made raisin-jack hit the spot quite nicely.[20]

PFC Donald Holzer of How Battery made one of the better finds at the artillery position near Garapan. In addition to a nice bunch of bananas, Holzer discovered a chicken that was running loose. Although

---
[18] Vice Admiral George Carrol Dyer, USN (Ret), The Amphibians Came To Conquer - The Story of Admiral Richard Kelly Turner, Volume II. (Washington: U.S. Government Printing Office, 1972). p. 872.
[19] James Tucker, Interview with author, September 11, 1992, Dubuque, Iowa.
[20] Multiple interviews at reunions of Third Battalion, Tenth Marines, 1992, Dubuque, Iowa.

the chicken was fortunate enough to escape the American shelling, it was not fortunate enough to escape the hungry Marine who had eaten nothing but combat rations for the longest time. After cleaning the chicken and getting a small fire started, Holzer filled his steel helmet with water and proceeded to boil the water, then add the chicken and a little later ate a delicious meal of boiled chicken with bananas for dessert.[21]

Action on the 5th of July was slow and the 3/10 Marines were able to establish a good position from which to provide artillery support. Due to the converging of units as a result of Saipan's contour, and because he wanted to give them a rest in preparation for the assault on Tinian, Lieutenant General Smith put the 2nd Division into a reserve status. However, the third and fourth battalions of the Tenth Marines were not as fortunate. These two units were formed into an artillery group of 105mm howitzers and under the group command of Lieutenant Colonel Jorgensen, CO of 4/10. They were attached to the 4th Division to provide fire support to the 23rd Marines.[22]

On the 5th of July, Japanese forces were falling back to mass themselves at Makunsha. Therefore, the 23rd Marines did not need all the artillery support anticipated and consequently 3/10 fired very little that evening. July 5th was also the day that Lieutenant General Smith decided to change the direction of attack of the 4th and 27th Divisions as a result of terrain and enemy resistance. At 0900 on the 6th the axis of advance was changed from northeast to north. Also, on the morning of 6 July, 3/10 received orders to make a reconnaissance for a new position forward.[23]

Because his battalion was in a good position and they could already range the northern tip of the island, Major Crouch opposed the unanticipated move. According to Corporal Marion Craig, the discussion became heated but to no avail as the 3/10 commanding officer was harshly ordered to make preparations and move when directed.[24]

---

[21] Donald Holzer, Interview with author, September 11, 1992, Dubuque, Iowa.
[22] Special Action Report, 10th Marines.
[23] Ibid.
[24] Marion Craig, Interview with author, August 3, 1990, Dubuque, Iowa.

Chapter 9

For all practical purposes, by the beginning of July the Japanese forces on Saipan were defeated. The massive firepower of United States forces from naval gunfire, air, and artillery, continually took a severe toll on the retreating Japanese. There was no way they could stop the Americans' attack and it was only a matter of time until there would be no-where else to retreat. A review of what the Japanese forces on Saipan endured in the first six months of 1944 better describes what their situation was when July arrived.

In early 1944, the Japanese were not certain that Saipan would be invaded, but all through the first 6 months of 1944 they still attempted to fortify their defenses on the island. However, United States Navy submarines wrecked havoc with Japanese ships attempting to transport steel and concrete mix to the island. Troop transports also fell prey to the underwater ships prowling the Western Pacific. As D-Day drew closer, the isolation of Saipan became so tight that when Lieutenant General Hideyoshi Obata, in charge of the 31st Army in the Marianas, was off conducting an inspection in the Palaus, he was unable to get back to Saipan. Responsibility for the defense of Saipan fell upon Lieutenant General Yoshitsuga Saito.[1]

Major Kiyoshi Yoshida was the intelligence officer of the 432nd Division Headquarters. Major Yoshida was captured on the 9th of July and provided some good insights into what the Japanese endured throughout the battle of Saipan and the developments that led to its terrible finish.[2]

On the 11th of June, the American aircraft of Vice Admiral Marc

---

[1] Henry I. Shaw, Jr., Bernard C. Nalty, and Edwin C. Turnbladh, History of U.S. Marine Corps Operations in WW II Central Pacific Drive, Volume III. (Washington: Historical Branch, G-3 Division, Headquarters, U.S. Marine Corps, 1966). p. 261.

[2] Major Yoshida, Kiyoshi, Intelligence officer of the former 43rd Division Headquarters, special interrogation of. Headquarters, Northern Troops and Landing Force, In the Field, 12 July 1944.

Mitschers powerful Task Force 58 bombed Saipan. The Japanese forces thought it to be nothing more than a routine attack, however, there was nothing routine about 200 aircraft swooping down on the Japanese airfield to destroy approximately 150 airplanes. This key blow assured the American forces of air supremacy for the duration of the campaign. At this time General Saito's command post was located in the village school house in Charan-Kanoa. The structure was a well-built wooden facility that had a concrete air raid shelter only 50 yards away as the command post was not bombproof.[3]

The 12th of June brought another United States air raid. The fact that the second raid was conducted the following day, and that it was carried out with increased intensity, made the Japanese feel certain that Saipan was to be the target of the next American invasion.[4]

Common sense dictated that the invasion of Saipan would be across the shores of Magicienne Bay on the eastern side of the island. The beaches of the large bay would best facilitate an amphibious landing by U. S. Marines. For this reason, the defense of the eastern sector of the island was entrusted to the 47th Mixed Brigade and the 9th Tank Regiment. Other responsibilities for Saipan's defense were assigned as follows: Northern Sector - 135th Infantry; Central Sector - 136th Regiment; Southern Sector - three independent infantry battalions, an artillery regiment, and the antiaircraft regiment.[5]

Another assault by Admiral Mitschers aircraft on June 13th would be the last massive airstrike on Saipan. The carriers moved off in search of a more lucrative target - the Japanese fleet. On the 14th of June, the naval gunfire ships of Admiral Jesse Oldendorf took over responsibility for softening up Saipan. Battleships, cruisers, and destroyers pounded the island in an effort to reduce the resistance the assaulting Marines would meet. Even though fire support was scattered around the island, the heaviest fire was placed on the beaches of Charan Kanoa. In addition, United States aircraft dropped propaganda leaflets on Charan Kanoa, thereby assuring the Japanese that at least some of the assault force would

---

[3] Ibid.
[4] Ibid.
[5] Shaw p. 260.

land there. However, General Saito could not be certain that there would not also be a landing at Magicienne Bay, so he had to leave a force there. Also, a diversionary maneuver in the Tanapag area well north of Charan Kanoa would force Lieutenant General Saito to keep the 135th Infantry Regiment in that area, which also relieved some of the resistance against the main assault across the beaches of Charan Kanoa.[6]

One thing that Lieutenant General Saito could be sure of was that his command post in the school house at Charan-Kanoa was to be untenable during the assault. From Charan-Kanoa Gen Saito moved to a cave that had a communications set up in place, as well as four 15cm guns emplaced. The cave was not large, only 15-20 feet in depth, but it was well defiladed to protect it from fire.

From this position Gen Saito ordered the tank attack against the 2nd Division the night of 16/17 June. Over thirty tanks attacked the Marines, but according to Major Yoshida the tanks took a wrong turn and instead of attacking along the coast road and into the Marines flank, they went directly into the middle of the Combat Team 2. Before the Japanese retreated northward, they lost 24 tanks, mostly to bazookas and anti-tank grenades.

By the 19th of June the Japanese forces were being pushed steadily backwards. They established a defensive line and dug in to protect Garapan from capture by the Marines. On this day Gen Saito moved his CP to the ridge directly above Chacha village. There was no prepared position here, but food had been stored and the huge rock slabs offered some protection against the murderous firepower of the United States Forces.

24 June was the day that Lieutenant General Saito was again forced to move his command post away from the pursuing Marines. The next location was described as an elaborate cave dug into one of the many sheer cliffs that was part of Mt Tapotchau. This location also had elaborate communications ability, but its location had a fatal flaw in that it was exposed to the naval gunfire from the sea. When United States ships pounded this location, many Japanese were killed and the communications gear was destroyed. However, on 27 June Gen Saito escaped to another location in an effort to stop the massive United States drive to capture Saipan.

---

[6] Ibid. p. 263.

The position that the Japanese ground commander on Saipan occupied on 27 June was not a good one. This location was described by the captured intelligence officer as the crudest of the group. The small cave was located just south of Radio Hill. This position like the others was soon found by the massive United States firepower and a beaten and battered Lieutenant Gen Saito made his final move on 30 June. This location was also a cave in a small valley, suggestively called the Valley of Hell by the Japanese. It was directly East of Makunsha Village near Hill 222.[7]

Testimony of another captured Japanese officer conflicts a little with the dates and locations of Gen Saito's moves. What is important to consider is that there were many moves for the Japanese leader caused by devastating fire from a relentless pursuer. It was a battered Japanese force that was being pushed back and quickly facing the hard realization that there was very little chance of any help arriving from Japan. Old General Saito was now confronted by the undeniable. His forces were beaten physically and their weapons were almost gone. The one thing they still had was their spirit and belief in the honor of dying for their emperor. After consulting with his officers on the 3rd of July, Lieutenant Saito made the inevitable decision that he and his forces go to their death in true Japanese Army fashion. They would abide by the SENJINKEN (Battle Ethics), "I will never suffer the disgrace of being taken alive," and "I will offer up the courage of my soul and calmly rejoice in living by the eternal principle."[8]

To put it in American terms, the Japanese knew they were licked, but they were going to go down fighting and take as many Americans with them as possible. In order to do this the Japanese would conduct a suicide attack against their foes. However, General Saito decreed that the assault must be more than a suicide attack to give one's life for his emperor. This attack must be a Gyokusai, which is an attack of such magnitude that it breaks the back of the enemy. To emphasize the ferocity he envisioned for the Gyokusai, Gen Saito spoke of "breaking the jewel." This expression referred to Japanese culture in which a jewel, a mirror, and a sword represent virtues that a nation should cultivate to live by. The sword stands

---

[7] Yoshida papers.
[8] Lieutenant General Saito's last message to Japanese officers and men defending Saipan, Confidential memo #15-44, Headquarters, Northern Troops and Landing Force, In the Field, 12 July, 1944.

Chapter 9

for firm decisive actions, wherein lies the true origin of all wisdom. The mirror represents seeing things as they are, good or bad, to determine true fairness and justice. The jewel, which Lieutenant Saito referred to, is the symbol of Japanese gentleness and piety. In declaring the breaking of the jewel, Gen Saito was disregarding the virtues of gentleness and piety, and exhorting his soldiers to find within themselves a ferocious fighting spirit that was unstoppable. * There could be nothing less if the Japanese forces were to break the Americans back. (Author's interpretation)

To do this the Japanese leader believed that each man must kill seven Americans before finally being killed himself. Prior to the final decision to conduct the Gyokusai, the Japanese established a password that told what they must do in the attack. "Seven lives to repay our country" was the password and inspiration for the Japanese.[9]

By the 4th of July, Lieutenant General Saito had dispatched officer messengers to all parts of Saipan in an effort to round up units to report to the General's position in preparation for the attack. However, this would prove to be easier said than done. Japanese forces were scattered about the island and communication between them was very limited. Because of this, it was very often a hit and miss situation as the messengers attempted to gather the remaining Japanese forces.

As units, groups, and even individual soldiers made their way to Makunsha, where the attack would begin, Lieutenant General Saito gave his farewell speech to his men. On the morning of 6 July at 0800, Gen Saito released his message to exert his men to accomplish their mission.

> "MESSAGE TO OFFICERS AND MEN DEFENDING SAIPAN"
>
> "I am addressing the officers and men of the Imperial Army on SAIPAN.
>
> For more than twenty days since the American Devils attacked, the officers, men, and civilian employees of the Imperial Army and Navy on this island have fought well and bravely. Everywhere they have demonstrated the honor and glory of the Imperial Forces. I expected that every man would do his duty.

---

[9] Ibid.

Heaven has not given us an opportunity. We have not been able to utilize fully the terrain. We have fought in unison up to the present time, but now we have no materials with which to fight and our artillery for attack has been completely destroyed. Our comrades have fallen one after another. Despite the bitterness of defeat, we pledge "Seven lives to repay our country."

The barbarous attack of the enemy is being continued. Even though the enemy has occupied only a corner of SAIPAN we are dying without avail under the violent shelling and bombing. Whether we attack or whether we stay where we are, there is only death. However, in death there is life. We must utilize this opportunity to exalt true Japanese manhood. I will advance with those who remain to deliver still another blow to the American Devils, and leave my bones on SAIPAN as a bulwark of the Pacific.

As it says in the "SENJINKUN" (Battle Ethics), "I will never suffer the disgrace of being taken alive," and "I will offer up the courage of my soul and calmly rejoice in living the eternal principle."

Here I pray with you for the eternal life of the Emperor and the welfare of the country and I advance to seek out the enemy."

"Follow me."[10]

With the conclusion of Gen Saito's speech there were many cries of Banzai throughout the Japanese ranks. This cry of exuberance and motivation was an expression of devotion and loyalty to their emperor. In simple terms, Banzai is translated as "Hail," or "Hail to the Emperor." While many people have been led to believe that Banzai is a type of suicide attack, that is not correct. Any soldier who ever heard the cry of Banzai from a charging Japanese soldier was only hearing the Japanese speak aloud in order to motivate himself for what he was doing.

Lieutenant General Saito's plan was intended to be The Last Great Banzai for himself and his men. It would be their last great hurrah as they paid honor to their emperor by conducting the

---

[10] Ibid.

Gyokusai and dying for him.[11]

The physical and mental stress of the Japanese predicament had taken its toll on Lieutenant General Saito. Even though his message to his soldiers had encouraged them to follow their general, he knew that he was in no condition to lead them into battle. According to the personal account of "The Last Days of Lieutenant General Saito" which was given by a captured Japanese officer to the NTLF G-2, "General Saito was feeling poorly because, for several days he had neither eaten nor slept well and was overstrained. He was wearing a long beard and was a pitiful sight."[12]

No one will ever know for certain when General Saito made the decision to commit suicide. However, on the evening of the 5th he was fed a dinner of canned crab meat. His schedule for the 6th was to give the message at 0800 and then perform the ceremonial suicide at 1000 in the small cave he was using for his command post. Although there are no eye witness accounts of the General's death, queried Japanese officers gave an account of how they were confident that the events transpired. First of all, the General would select a special place in the cave and after cleaning this space himself he sat down facing the East. As he held his own sword in front of him he called out the expression, 'Tenno Heika. Banzai' (Hurrah for the Emperor).

Lieutenant General Saito then drew his own blood. Within moments the General's trusted adjutant used the Generals own pistol to shoot him in his right temple. Almost immediately thereafter the adjutant committed suicide, as well as the other Shamboes (Japanese staff officers). Before the day was over the body of General Saito was cremated, but all through the day and night of 6 July the soldiers of Japan were making preparations to carry out their orders.[13]

The accounts of General Saito's last days are from previously classified records of Lieutenant General H. M. Smith headquarters. As was noted, the testimony given by the captured Japanese to their interrogators

---

[11] Authors interpretation of Japanese tradition based on: Kurt Singer, Mirror, Sword, & Jewel, (London: Croom Helm, 1973). p.11.
[12] Captured Japanese officer's personal account of "The Last Days of Lieutenant General Saito." File #5450-30-5, Headquarters, Northern Troops and Landing Force, In the Field, 14 July, 1944.
[13] Ibid.

was one of conjecture. However, it was given within days of the event.

In 1965, Don Jones, a former Marine who served on Saipan, sought out and found Captain Sakae Oba, who fought in and survived the Gyokusai. Rather than commit suicide, Captain Oba chose to fight on and for eighteen months led his small group of soldiers and civilians as they evaded and harassed the American forces on Saipan. While on Saipan, Jones knew of Oba's exploits from personal experience since he had nearly been killed one day in an ambush by Oba. He never forgot his fascination with the renegade Japanese captain and so, over twenty years later, Jones located and interviewed Captain Oba and wrote a book about his experiences on Saipan. In Jones' book, <u>OBA, THE LAST SAMURAI</u>, the Japanese officer expounded on what earlier documents said by describing how Gen Saito did not commit suicide alone. With him were Admiral Nagumo, at that time head of the combined navy in the Marianas, Brigadier General Igeta, and Rear Admiral Yano. The four senior officers dined on squid and rice in addition to the crab meat and they toasted with sake. All four officers were dressed in their best uniforms for the occasion. After saying their prayers, each stabbed himself and was then finished by a shot to the head.[14] The exact details of Gen Saito's death are almost insignificant when compared to the magnitude of the Gyokusai he had ordered.

The day of 6 July found preparations ongoing for the attack. As attempts were made to organize the attack, after darkness fell the Japanese probed the lines of the American forces before them. These forces were the men of the 27th Army Division. The Japanese probing paid off as they discovered a large area from which they were never fired on. This was obviously a weakness in the American defense that could be exploited.[15]

---

[14] Don Jones, Oba, The Last Samuri - Saipan 1944-45, (Novato, California: Presidio Press, 1986). pp. 64-65.
[15] Ibid. p. 71.

1. The landing beach where the U.S. Marines first assaulted the island of Saipan on June 15, 1944.

2. An aerial view of the Western shore of Saipan where American forces conducted the main assault for the invasion of Saipan.

3. Soon after arriving ashore, Lt. Gen. H.M. Smith met with his staff to appraise the situation.

4. Marines take a break during a lull in the action. Mt. Tapochau looms in the background.

5. A Marine 105mm howitzer blasts away at Japanese forces to the northwest. This was the howitzer used to fire directly on the massive suicide attack.

6. A small locomotive was used, before the Japanese invasion, to haul loads of sugarcane from the fields to processing factories.

7. This train track, built to move sugar cane, was used by the Japanese to help guide their suicide directly into the artillery batteries of 3/10 during the predawn hours of July 7, 1944.

8. Dug in howitzers provided more protection for gun and crew.

9. A marine forward observer team calling for artillery fire on enemy targets.

10. Supporting arms fire devastated Garapan but infantry units still had to go in to root out small pockets of resistance.

11. July 8, 1944, witnessed the results of the terrible carnage resulting from the massive Japanese attack against U.S. Army and Marine forces the previous day. Some Japanese attackers were reportedly armed only with sticks during the attack.

12. Another picture revealing the terrible slaughter that was necessary to stop the fanatical Japanese suicide attack against American forces on Saipan.

13. This gulch was filled with dead Japanese soldiers, and at least one Japanese officer, as suggested by the officer's sword in the middle of the photo.

Chapter 10

The 27th Division attacked northward on July 6th, on the western side of the island of Saipan. The 105th regiment was on the left against the ocean shoreline and the 165th was on the right in the foothills that protruded out from the mountain range. The 106th regiment was behind the 105th and 165th as the division reserve. By the end of the day on the 6th, the 105th regiment found itself about 900 yards past road junction 2, or just over 1000 yards from their objective of Makunsha. The 2nd Battalion of Major McCarthy established a defensive position in the regiment's left sector against the coast. A two-company front was established between the coast road and the railroad tracks with two sentries placed out on the beach to watch that area. The left flank of the left company and the right flank of the right company were curved back to the rear to protect each companies' exposed flank. This created a horseshoe type of formation for the second battalion.

Not long after the second battalion was in position, the first battalion came up on its right. Lieutenant Colonel O'Brien, CO of the 1st Bn, and Major McCarthy agreed that the 1st Bn would tie in with 2nd Bn to establish its position for the evening. With the 2nd on his left Lieutenant Colonel O'Brien was not very concerned with that flank, however, to better secure his right flank there was almost a whole company bent around to the right to protect that side. Lieutenant Colonel O'Brien's concern for the right flank of his battalion was justified as there was 300 yards of open ground between 1st Bn and the unit on its right, the 3rd Bn of the 105th. The cause of this gap was the problem created by Japanese resistance in Harakiri Gulch that the 3rd Bn had to deal with. For whatever reason, the fact remained that as evening came upon the regiment there was a 300-yard gap in its line.

The company on the left of the 3rd Bn was G Company. It was attached, from the 2nd Bn, to the 3rd Bn for the operation. Lieutenant

Colonel OBrien's reason for not tying in with the 3rd Bn was that he was concerned that he would overextend, and therefore weaken his line. In addition to this, the ground was very open and the battalion commander felt it could be covered by fire, even though there were no soldiers physically occupying the ground.

It was about 2000, the evening of the 6th, when a Japanese soldier was found sleeping along the side of the road near the 3rd Bn, 105th headquarters. After much interrogation, the "leading seaman" of the 55th Guard Force made it known that an all-out attack by all remaining Japanese on the island had been ordered by Lieutenant General Saito. In light of receiving this word, Lieutenant Colonel OBrien naturally became even more concerned about the large gap on his right. Lieutenant Colonel OBrien went up the chain of command to request more troops to fill in the gap, but the 27th Division HQ responded that there were no men available and the 1st BN of the 105th Regiment would have to make do with what it had.[1]

As the Japanese had been doing their patrolling and probing of the American lines, it was from this large gap between the 1st and 3rd Battalions of the 105th, that the Japanese probes received no fire. This told the Japanese that this area would be one location they would definitely assault when the attack began. Although he had no way of being sure of it at the time, Lieutenant Colonel OBrien's fears of the vulnerability of that gap were well founded.

With the knowledge that Japanese troops would most likely be assembling near Makunsha, heavy artillery firing pounded the area. Captured Japanese soldiers later admitted that the artillery fire was instrumental in breaking up the attack formations and therefore delayed the time of the assault. Unfortunately, it was not able to break the will of the Japanese and prevent the inevitable.[2]

It was close to 0400, on the morning of 7 July, when the tremendous wave of Japanese rolled into the lines of the 105th Regiment. The senior Japanese officer to actually lead the attack was the commander

---

[1] Edmund G. Love, The 27th Infantry Division in World War II, (Washington: Infantry Journal Press, 1949). p. 436.
[2] Ibid. p. 436.

of the 135th Infantry Regiment, Colonel Eisuke Suzuki. Although there was tremendous confusion at the time, the attack developed along three main avenues of assault. A small force of undetermined size moved down the coast road with two tanks in support. This attack moved by the two sentries on the beach and past the left flank of the 2nd Bn with little resistance and continued down the road. The largest attack force surged down the railroad track that ran between the 1st and 2nd Battalions, while the third Japanese assault drove directly through the large gap that existed in the regiment's lines between 1st and 3rd Battalions. As some of the Japanese attacked the soldiers on each side of the gap between the two battalions, hundreds of others swept through and continued their unimpeded attack down the Tanapag Plain. The plans that existed to cover the gap by fire became impossible to execute as every soldier was required to fight for his life against the tremendous onslaught to his immediate front. The magnitude of this attack was unlike anything seen previously in the war. The most famous description of the attack was given by the commanding officer of the 2nd Bn. In a memorandum Major McCarthy wrote: "It was like the movie stampede staged in the old Wild West movies. We were the cameraman. These Japanese just kept coming and coming and didn't stop. It didn't make any difference if you shot one; five more would take his place. We would be in the foxholes looking up, as I said, just like those cameramen used to be. The Japanese ran right over us."[3]

---

[3] Ibid. p. 443.

Chapter 11

As he had been ordered to do, Major Crouch instructed his battalion to begin its displacement from their recently occupied position east of Garapan. The move began after noontime toward the battalion's newly assigned area.[1] As always, the orders from regiment designated a large area which the battalion should occupy. Within this area the battalion headquarters would direct sub-areas which the batteries would occupy, but it was up to the battery commander to determine the exact position where he would lay in his gun line.

Because it was late in the afternoon and the men felt that this was not a necessary move, the battalion did not execute the move with the greatest sense of urgency. After all, the Japanese were licked and this was just a token move anyway, so they thought.[2] Normally when the battalion moved to a new position, there were certain essential firing personnel that always went in as the advance party, followed closely by the main body. Later, the rest of the logistics and support personnel would follow and join up with the unit. Typically, these men may be supply, mess, maintenance, or administration Marines whose job was vital to the functioning of the artillery battalion, but not a requirement for firing the howitzers. However, on this move Marines of every battery function participated in the initial move. Cooks and clerks went forward to learn about and take part in what was required for the occupation and preparation of a new position.[3]

The ability to communicate is a critical requirement for an artillery unit to perform its mission. Normally, the battalion communication officer went forward to oversee the setup and activation of all communication. On

---

[1] Special Action Report, Headquarters, Tenth Marines, Second Marine Division, Fleet Marine Force, In the Field, 22 July 1944.
[2] Multiple interviews at reunions of Third Battalion, Tenth Marines, 1990 and 1992, Dubuque, Iowa.
[3] Wilber J. Buss, Interview with author, August 3, 1990, Dubuque, Iowa.

this particular move however, Lieutenant Wilber Buss was asked by his communication chief, Staff Sergeant Lea Bell, if he could take the battalions communication forward and take responsibility for its setup and operation. Staff Sergeant Bell was a former Marine raider and according to Buss was "a pretty sharp character." Although the communication officer had faith in his communication chief, he still felt it important to check with the commanding officer. After Major Crouch gave his thumbs up to the suggestion, Lieutenant Buss told Bell that he could go forward with the advance CP and that he himself would stay with the rear echelon.[4]

Based on all the considerations of mission, enemy, and terrain, 3/10 had been ordered to locate itself on the map location of TA 247 M,R,&W and TA 237 B & C. This area had decent roads moving into the area which allowed easy access for the firing batteries. It also allowed the big 105's to easily range Marpi Point on the northern tip of the island. During their displacement forward, the men of 3/10 were surprised to find themselves moving forward of the Pack 75 howitzers of the 1st and 2nd Battalions. Normally the smaller, shorter ranged howitzers were positioned forward of the 105's.[5]

As the battalion left its position east of Garapan and moved toward its newly designated location, it headed in a northeasterly direction. The artillery convoys traveled on a road along the bottom of the mountain range across foothills which served as the eastern edge of the Tanapag Plain. The road continued along the bottom of the foothills until it reached the target area of 237D. At this point it junctioned with another road that ran almost north and south, thereby creating a T intersection. The southern road went up into the mountains while the northern road descended down a gentle sloping hill and crossed a railroad track; then, it continued another 400 yards until it met the coastal Tanapag Road at Road Junction 5. RJ 5 was located several hundred yards southwest of the small coastal town of Tanapag. The narrow railroad track the road intersected ran from the sugarcane fields of the Tanapag Plain to the sugar refinery south at Charan-Kanoa, near the location where 3/10 had landed.

The battalion was still in support of the 4th Division, which was

---

[4] Ibid.
[5] Special Action Report, Tenth Marines.

located to the east of 3/10 and driving north toward Marpi Point. As a result of this, the positions of the batteries within the battalion area would form an echelon right in order to facilitate their general direction of fire to the northeast and Marpi Point.[6]

How Battery occupied the northern-most position and, therefore, the left side of the battalion echelon. Because the battery commander and executive officer were not in the Garapan position when the order came down to displace, 1st Lieutenant Hal Lane led Battery H into its position approximately 100 yards southeast of RJ 5. The gunline was established on the edge of the tree-line about 20 yards east of, and parallel to, the north-south road that ended at RJ 5. The area in front of the gunline was just low scrub brush, but running diagonally in front of the howitzers were trees that lined the bank of a six feet deep stream bed. These trees were about 80 to 100 yards to the left front of gun 4. Visibility to the other side of the stream bed was blocked by the trees. No survey had been put into the position yet, so a reference direction was determined from the direction of the railroad on the map. Lieutenant Lane oriented his aiming circle with the direction of the railroad tracks that also ran diagonally in front of the gunline from the right side. Then Lane turned the aiming circle toward gun 1 and began to lay the howitzers. From his position in front of the gunline, between the howitzers and the railroad track, Lieutenant Lane had just finished laying gun 1 when he began to receive sniper fire. After he quickly moved back behind the relative safety of the gunline, gun 1 proceeded to lay the other three guns using the reciprocal direction method.[7]

Headquarters and Service Battery established a forward command post and fire direction center only about 150 yards southwest of, and across the road from the How position. This command post consisted mostly of a large general-purpose tent in which the forward communications center was located. This tent also contained the battalion FDC, which computed the data for each of the firing batteries to put on their guns to fire on enemy targets.[8]

---

[6] Author's map study of Saipan.
[7] Harold A. Lane, "Recollections of the 10th Marines," March, 1990, Santa Rosa, California, p. 13.
[8] Dodd Sellers, "As I Recall: Remembering 1941-1946," March 12, 1991, Tuscaloosa,

The intersection of the road and the railroad tracks was where Item Battery established its position. The gunline was laid parallel to the road on the west side to facilitate its line of fire to the northeast. From the distant left front, or north, the railroad tracks ran southwest and crossed the road just to the left of the gunline and continued on to the batteries rear. Because much of the plain was low lying enough to be marshy during the rainy season, the railroad was built upon a high berm, which prevented Item Battery from seeing much of the area immediately on the other side. Another obstacle that not only obscured Items vision, but also hindered its ability to shoot was a large tree to the front of the gunline. A couple of strong Marines with sharp axes took care of the tree. Just 50 yards behind the gunline a drainage ditch ran through a culvert in the railroad berm.[9]

The George Battery position was the southernmost position of the battalion, to the right of the echelon. George was also the battery that occupied the highest terrain. It set in on the high ground just before the T road junction that the other batteries would pass through to get to their positions. The best spot for the howitzers within this location was on the left side of the road they traveled to get there, but short of the north-south road that led down the hill to the other battery positions. Between the road and the gunline was a large pile of big timbers that may have been placed there to be used later as railroad ties. Beside and below the gunline was a long natural berm that overlooked the railroad and another area behind the Item Battery gunline. On this berm, to the front of the gunline about 60 yards, was a small abandoned shack.[10]

By the time the batteries reached their respective positions that evening darkness was quickly approaching. After the gunline had been properly laid in on the azimuth of fire other standard procedures of occupation were carried out. Local security was established as listening posts were put out in front of the gunline. Security was enhanced by the positioning of .50 caliber machine guns. However, by their own admission, many of the Marines that evening were not as diligent as they should have been as they dug in and prepared their positions. After all,

---

Alabama, p. 42.
[9] Allen Ball, Letter to author, March 4, 1992, Bakersfield, California.
[10] Multiple interviews with members of G Battery, September 12, 1992, Dubuque, Iowa.

nothing had happened to dispel the rumor that the Japanese were on the run and practically defeated. It was somewhat of a surprise when the Marines on watch that night heard the sounds of a battle well to the northeast of their position about 0330 on the 7th. No one knew exactly what to make of it, but no one really cared as the veterans of three weeks of intense fighting were used to the sounds of battle. Very few of the men who were sleeping at the time were even awakened by the weapons fire and explosions.[11]

The closest unit in 3/10 to the ongoing battle was How Battery, and the Marines of Battery H really did not give the noise of the distant battle a second thought. But unbeknownst to these men, while the distant storm at sea was arousing little more than a casual curiosity a silent tidal wave was fast approaching their position.

Once the Japanese had passed through the 105th lines there was nothing in their way for nearly 1000 yards. The breakthrough was so successful that the advancing Japanese force was able to maintain a semblance of formation as they continued on their southwest axis of advance along the Tanapag Plain toward Garapan. The continuing battle to their rear also aided the Japanese advance as the noise of the distant battle covered any noise made by the attacking force approaching How Battery and the rest of 3/10.[12]

---

[11] Multiple interviews with members of H Battery, September 12, 1992, Dubuque, Iowa.
[12] Author's summary of existing conditions that evening and early morning.

Chapter 12

It was not until the Japanese were about 600 yards in front of the How Battery gunline that they were noticed; and then the Marines were not sure whether it was friendly or enemy forces approaching their position. According to 1st Lieutenant Arnold Hostetter, XO of How Battery, "...about 0515, just as it was getting light, a group of men were seen advancing on the battery position from the right front at about 600 yards. It was thought that Army troops were somewhere to the front, so fire on this group was held until they were definitely identified as Japanese at about 400 yards. We knew that our men manning listening posts were somewhere to our front so the firing battery was ordered to open fire with time and ricochet fire on the group to the right. Firing was also heard from the machineguns on the left..."[1]

The streambed and tree-line to How Battery's left created a problem because visibility to the other side was totally blocked. Directly to the front of the gunline the visibility was good for hundreds of meters, and to the right was Item Battery. To the battery rear was H&S Battery and then 4/10, so the area to which How was most vulnerable was the left. Complicating the lack of visibility to the other side of the tree-line was the coastal highway coming from the northeast. Considering all these factors the battery placed all four of its .50 caliber machineguns just on the other side of the tree-line to cover the open plain and coast road to the north and northeast.[2]

The four machineguns were placed almost equal distant apart and oriented in a northeasterly direction. On the weapon farthest from the road was PFC Ben Hokit. Hokit was able to hear the noise of the fighting to the northeast, however, things were very quiet and very dark immediately to

---

[1] Carl Hoffman, Major, USMC, Saipan: The Beginning of the End, (Washington: Historical Division, Headquarters, United States Marine Corps, 1950, p. 224.
[2] Multiple interviews with members of H Battery, September 12, 1992, Dubuque, Iowa.

their front. However, PFC James Dent, one of the other Marines on the gun with Hokit, was not at all satisfied that things were as quiet as they seemed. Even though he believed he was hearing something almost all the time, shortly before dawn was to start breaking, Dent suddenly became adamant that he heard noises coming from down in the streambed located behind them. Hokit told Dent that he had no authority to allow it, but if Dent was so sure that he heard noises in the streambed, maybe he should fire a round into that area just to satisfy his own concerns. After hearing that, Dent put his carbine to his shoulder, pointed it down into the streambed and fired one round. One round was all it took. In the darkness of the early morning the little bit of light provided by the muzzle blast of Dent's carbine was enough to clearly illuminate many Japanese soldiers moving through the gully. As quickly as they could, the men began to fire on the Japanese with their carbines. Also, with Hokit and Dent was PFC Richard Hopkins, who quickly scrambled out of the machinegun pit they were in to grab the .50 caliber weapon and turn it around so that it faced the streambed. As quickly as he accomplished this, Hopkins cut loose with a hellacious rate of fire into the enemy infested area. For several minutes Hopkins continued to fire the machinegun into the streambed until he was killed by the Japanese. As he saw Hopkins slumped over, Hokit jumped in behind the machinegun and continued the firing. It was not long before Hokit observed that the tracers coming out of the weapon were no longer going straight, but beginning to curve as they left the barrel. The barrel was becoming so worn that it no longer shot straight. This was of little consequence as shortly thereafter the machinegun "froze up" and would no longer fire. Hokit was now very vulnerable to the Japanese fire so he dove forward and down into the machinegun pit. No sooner had he landed in the muddy hole than a Japanese grenade landed beside him. With the butt of his carbine, Hokit pushed the grenade deep into the mud and then placed the wooden stock of the weapon over the grenade. Hokits quick thinking saved his life as the grenade's explosion did little injury to him. Realizing that he was not in a very good position, Hokit moved away from that gun and toward the adjacent one. As he arrived at the next machinegun, Hokit found it unoccupied but ready for firing. After expending the belt of ammo that was in the weapon, he removed the back plate to make it inoperable. Then he began working his way toward the battery.[3]

PFCs Donald Holzer and Harold Hoffman were also on one of the How Battery .50 caliber machineguns that early morning. Its location was slightly elevated above the surrounding terrain and therefore they had a fairly good view of the area during the light of day. The area they were positioned in was clear of brush, but within a few yards behind them the vegetation became very thick with four feet high heavy weeds and brush turning into heavy trees with thick undergrowth at the bottom of the trees that lined the streambed. While it was still dark, the two Marines heard a lot of firing and other commotion to their right and rear, but did not think it would affect them so quickly. Suddenly they noticed three Japanese behind them and some others off to their right. Holzer and Hoffman quickly dove into the high weeds closest to them. When it appeared that a Japanese passing close by saw Holzer, he attempted to shoot the enemy but his carbine jammed so the Marine was forced to butt-stroke the enemy. As Holzer and Hoffman observed how many Japanese were now in their immediate area the two started to move back through the heavy vegetation toward the battery position. As they did, they ran into two other Japanese and were forced to use their knives at such close quarters. As they continued toward the battery gunline the two Marines ran out of cover and had to cross the streambed, but it was full of Japanese. The streambed at this location was approximately five feet deep but twelve feet across. They could not stay where they were, so they had to count on the advantage of darkness and surprise to get them across. Running as fast as they could travel was not enough. The two were spotted and taken under fire. Holzer was hit in the shoulder but able to keep running, but Hoffman was hit in the back and killed.[4]

Private Armand Masse was on the .50 caliber machinegun closest to the road. He had not slept much that night and therefore heard the distant gunfire since early in the morning. Masse was startled when one of the guns to his right started, "...to blast off," while it was still too dark to see very well. However, before much time elapsed Masse was able to see

---

[3] Ben Hokit, Interview with author, September 12, 1992, Dubuque, Iowa.
[4] Donald Holzer, Interview with author, September 12, 1992, Dubuque, Iowa.

many Japanese approaching his position as well. The Marines opened up on the attacking Japanese and cut them down. It seemed to Masse that the Japanese attack would fade after a heavy burst of gunfire, then materialize again quickly. While his attention was mostly focused to his front Masse did not miss the distinct noise of a truck or tank moving down the road to his left. Although the Marines were able to keep their weapon in action and repel the attack none of them escaped without being seriously wounded. After the main thrust of the attack seemed to be over some Japanese continued to pass near the machinegun position that Masse and the others still occupied. As they were seriously injured and out of ammo, the Marines had no recourse but to play dead. Fortunately, they were not bothered by any passing Japanese. After a while Masse heard the voice of his good buddy, Jimmy Dent. As he was moving along the gunline toward the road Dent came upon the position and saw that one of the Marines was still alive. Private Ernie Marusco had also survived and was talking to Dent. After helping Marusco, Dent assisted Masse out of their hole and stated that they had to get out of there. The three men started out very slowly toward the road. Due to the severity of their wounds, Masse and Marusco could not move very fast. After reaching the road the three crossed and continued in the same direction toward the beach. At this point, Marusco told Masse to pass him as they moved along. Once they reached the beach they headed south and had to cross the gulley where the streambed ran into the ocean. As Dent assisted Masse in climbing up the small streambank the two noticed that Marusco was not with them. The brave Marine, from Brewster, New York, who had lied about his age to get into the Marine Corps, died before they arrived at the streambed. With Masse's arm around Dent for support, the two continued south between the road and water until they were spotted by a jeep on the road that took them to safety.[5]

It was soon after the machineguns opened up that the battery first observed the movement to the distant front. As the advancing force got closer the men of H Battery could hardly believe their eyes. There was supposed to be an infantry regiment to their front, yet a large Japanese force was coming directly at them. The attacking force was able to

---

[5] Armand Masse, Letter to author, December 5, 1992, Lowell, Massachusetts.

virtually maintain a traditional attack formation with officers at the front in dress uniforms and swords drawn. The order was sent to the gunline to prepare to open fire with time fuzes set to .4 seconds. Initial rounds were fired at the command of the XO pit; but, even as the direct fire into them devastated the initial ranks of Japanese troops, they continued to attack. As the suicidal Japanese assault drew closer the command was given for the guns to fire at will. There was now no time to set fuzes as the Japanese pressed closer to the gunline. Screaming and yelling, the fanatical Japanese continued their advance. Whatever round was readily available was fired. By now the Japanese were close enough that the cannoneers depressed the howitzer muzzles in order to make the rounds explode in the ground in front of the Japanese so that the resulting explosion would disperse more as it ricocheted into them.[6]

At some time as the gunline opened fire, some of the cannoneers wondered about the fate of the battery security out in front of the gunline. The men knew very well that several battery security positions were located directly to the front of the gunline and in their line of fire. Many of the Marines within the gun position had been in those forward positions just a few hours before the Japanese attack hit the battery. One of those men was Corporal Kenneth Dondero. As he realized the magnitude of the Japanese attack, Dondero was fearful that all in those forward positions would be killed, but that was not the case.[7]

In a foxhole forward of gun 3 were PFC Edward Anderson, PFC John Zikowski, and PFC Joseph Galinas. All three were found shot in the face and head, still manning their listening post.[8]

Much more fortunate were the three Marines to their right in a security position to the front of gun one. PFCs Walter M. Campbell, Robert L. Kelly, and Wayne. C Shepard survived the onslaught as not many Japanese moved over their position. The one big exception to this was the time when four Japanese jumped simultaneously into the large bomb crater the three Marines occupied as a foxhole. Since the Japanese were not aware they were lying in the crater, the three Marines quickly

---

[6] Ralph Mills, Interview with author, August 3, 1990 and September 11, 1992, Dubuque, Iowa.
[7] William Dondero, Interview with author, September 12, 1992, Dubuque, Iowa.
[8] Multiple interviews with members of H Battery, September 11, 1992, Dubuque, Iowa.

shot all four. Ironically, about 30 minutes later one of the enemy soldiers regained consciousness and suddenly attempted to choke PFC Kelly. Three more bullets in the enemy killed him for good. It would be many more hours that these three would be forced to remain in this location, literally surrounded at times by the enemy until American forces could assure their safety.[9]

Oddly enough, the crazed Japanese attackers bypassed a second fighting hole in the brush out in front of the How Battery gunline that early July 7th morning. By staying low and staying quiet and being a little selective about which enemy soldiers they shot, PFCs Harold Lieber, Lloyd A. Derose, and Gilbert L. McElroy also survived the Japanese onslaught. On occasion the Marines were forced to shoot Japanese who came near their position in order to get water and weapons from the passing enemy.[10]

The security position on the right flank of gun one was not unnoticed by the attackers. Corporal Richard Czekala and PFC Edward Cosby were killed in foxholes as they defended the right flank of the gunline.[11]

---

[9] Sergeant Stanford Opotowsky, USMC Combat Correspondent, "We're All Infantrymen," Leatherneck, January, 1945, p. 63.
[10] Ibid.
[11] Multiple interviews with members of H Battery, September 11, 1992, Dubuque, Iowa.

Chapter 13

On the gunline that morning were many instances of Marines standing to fight in the face of overwhelming odds. PFC Lester Hobach drove a radio jeep that was parked off the gunline behind gun four. He was asleep in his foxhole that morning when he and the radio operator woke up to the sound of machine gun fire. Shortly after Hobach heard the .50 cals on the battery left begin firing the howitzers began to blast away. As he looked out ahead of the guns Hobach saw many Japanese soldiers attacking toward them. As the two Marines watched the action to the battery front, Japanese began to flank the left side of the battery and PFC Hobach and the radio operator became carbine operators as they fired on enemy soldiers advancing on the gunline from the left. A short while later in the morning, as the position became untenable, Hobach and the other Marine started to fall back across the road but the radio operator was killed. As Hobach hit the deck in an area of very heavy bushes next to the road he hugged the ground tightly as a machinegun fired its ammo just over his head. Not exactly sure what to do at the moment, he just lay there as the machinegun cut off so many leaves above him that he was practically covered as they fell.[1]

Corporal Earl Schoenker clearly heard the sound of a tank moving down the road behind the gunline. Not in his wildest dream did he expect a Japanese tank to be so close to his position, so Schoenker immediately "assumed it was an American tank coming back from the front to a rest area in the rear." Only after the tank was directly behind the gun section did the Marines hear the men sitting on the tank speaking Japanese. When it was apparent that it was a Japanese tank, there still wasn't the realization that an all-out attack was occurring. The initial impression by Schoenker and others was that this lone tank had broken the front lines and penetrated

---

[1] Lester Hobach, Cassette tape to author, 1989, Canton, Ohio.

to the artillery battalion position. Suddenly someone directed his attention to the field directly in front of the gun line. Schoenker saw what seemed like thousands of screaming Japanese attacking their position. At that moment there was no longer any doubt that they were caught up in a full-scale suicide attack.[2]

The tank had moved further down the road as Corporal Schoenker and the others fired their 105millimeter howitzer into the oncoming hordes. As they shot and killed the attacking Japanese, more and more would continue to advance over and around the bodies of their fallen comrades. Some Japanese were now close enough to put accurate small arms fire into the H gunline from the front, and Marines started to fall near their howitzers from the Japanese fire. In addition, many Japanese were beginning to flank the How gunline and the fire was becoming so heavy that cannoneers had to fire the howitzers from a low stoop, or crawl, position.[3]

The gunner on gun 1 was Corporal Ellis Oscar Palm, known to his Marine buddies as E.O. One of his reasons for joining the Marine Corps was that he did not want to fight in the cold of Northern Europe. However, he never expected how hot things would get that early morning of 7 July. Corporal Palm had phone duty for his gun section from midnight to 0400. The duty consisted of wearing the headphones that were wired into the other guns and the executive officers pit so all guns could receive firing data to set on the howitzers if they were required to shoot. Standing duty with Palm was PFC Frank Marshall. Like the other sections, gun one responded to the attack with direct fire from their howitzer into the attacking Japanese. And like the other guns, it seemed as if no matter how many Japanese they killed more continued appearing. As with the other end of the gunline, the right side of How Battery was swarming with Japanese. After several men in the section had been killed or wounded, the Marines of gun 1, led by their section chief, Sergeant Robert Pace, started to abandon their howitzer as ordered and move in toward gun 2 and the center of the battery position. Corporal Palm took the firing lock out of the breech block and was starting toward gun 2 when Sergeant Pace returned.

---

[2] Earl Schoenker, Cassette tape to author, 1989, Steeleville, Illinois.
[3] Multiple interviews with members of H Battery, September 11, 1992, Dubuque, Iowa.

The section chief had run into the battery commander, Captain Harold Nelson, who instructed Sergeant Pace to take his section back to their gun and attempt to destroy the Japanese tanks moving down the road behind the gunline. Guns 4, 3, and 2 had enough trees between them and the tank on the road that neither could fire at the other. However, gun one had a clear shot to the road as the trees thinned out to the southern end of the position.

Corporal Palm initially protested the instructions saying they did not have a chance. But, as Sergeant Pace repeated the order the two of them, followed by PFC Eric Johnson and Corporal Clifford Dogget, moved to the howitzer to prepare it for firing. As the 105millimeter howitzer was swung around to the rear it was necessary to tip over 55 gallon drums the section had put to the front of the gun for protection. While Johnson and Dogget manned the howitzer as gunner and number one man respectively, Palm loaded and Sergeant Pace directed fire. Even though it was just getting light enough, the Marines could clearly see two tanks on the road. After firing five or six quick shots at the two tanks, Corporal Palm felt confident they got them both.[4] As the four Marines again started to abandon the gun, Sergeant Pace was doubled over by a shot to the stomach, but managed to move away toward gun 2 again.[5] Corporal Johnson was also shot and fell over dead at the howitzer.[6] The following day found the one tank still dead in its tracks where the four Marines on gun one destroyed it. The other moved on down the road.

PFC William Miller was one of the ammo men on gun 1. As the action was fast and furious that morning there was little time to stop and ponder the moment. Miller was busy preparing ammo for firing when he was knocked down with a gunshot wound. As he lay there having his wound attended by the corpsman, Doc Robeson, it became apparent that things were not well in the battery. A short while later as he regained his strength, Miller got to his feet to go back on the howitzer. As he did, he witnessed his good friend Eric Johnson shot and killed. It was not long afterward that the word came from the XO pit to fall back. As Miller

---

[4] Ellis O. Palm, Letter to author, February, 1990, Baudette, Minnesota.
[5] Ibid.
[6] William Miller, Interview with author, September 11, 1992, Dubuque, Iowa.

started to move back toward the road his last observation of the gunline was Doc Robeson treating another wounded man. Unfortunately, that would be the last man the courageous corpsman would ever treat as Robeson was shot and killed applying a bandage to the wounded Marine. As Miller arrived at the road behind the battery position he came upon the Japanese tank on the road. The tank was not firing at the time and Miller was close enough that, "I could see through the firing slot and see his "beady" little eyes looking out." Miller did not stay there looking too long as he crossed the road seeking a safer location.[7]

On gun 3 that morning were several Marines sitting there talking. Two of them were brothers with Corporal Ralph Mills being a few years older than his little brother, PFC Julian B. Mills, or JB as they all called him. JB was a member of gun section 2, but just happened to be at Corporal Jack Anderson's gun section 3 talking that early morning when the Japanese hit. As the fire mission was being received on gun 3 the talking Marines were joined by other members of the gun crew: PFCs James Worsley, Carl Leonhardt, and James Tikal. The initial fire command sent to the gun directed that the charges be cut to something less than a full charge seven. As the approaching forces were recognized as Japanese, the men fired several volleys at the command of the XO pit. However, as the enemy attacked closed with the How Battery gun line the men began to fire at will with a full charge 7 fired with each shot. As the cannoneers poured round after round of whatever projectile was available into the Japanese, the Japanese attackers kept coming. With sufficient men on the gun to fire at the Japanese attackers, PFC Worsley grabbed his carbine and dropped to the ground and began firing at the approaching enemy. After the word was received from the XO pit to fall back, Corporal Anderson passed on the word to the men in his section that instructions were given to fall back. Being on the inside of the gunline, gun 3 was not taking the heavy fire that the flank pieces were and Corporal Mills said he wanted to stay on the howitzer and keep firing. Corporal Anderson gave his consent and PFC Mills and PFC Worsley asked to stay with Corporal Mills and keep firing also. As Worsley did a great job of killing the Japanese in close proximity of their howitzer, the two Mills brothers were firing the howitzer

---

[7] Ibid.

at the most lucrative target they could see. To the front of gun 3, Corporal Mills noticed a place along the tree-line where a large number of Japanese where located. Mills fired a round into them. However, the Japanese continued their attack and gun 3 was soon a very dangerous place to be as bullets flew everywhere. One of these bullets hit the precision machined edge of the howitzers breech block as it was open while another shell was being loaded. The resulting nick of the bullet prevented the closure of the breech, which prevented further firing. This was just as well as Worsley and the Mills brothers realized that they better leave the position while they could. As the three Marines started to fall back, Corporal Mills gave the breech block a hard kick and sent it slamming shut. After firing the final round, he too went back through the trees behind the gunline toward the road. As he approached the road, Corporal Mills encountered and quickly shot a Japanese soldier. After crossing the road and entering the wooded area on the other side he came upon the position where many of the Marines had congregated amongst a lot of crates that held what appeared to be airplane parts. Not satisfied that this was the place he wanted to be and not knowing that his brother JB was in the position, the older Mills left the area and moved into a thickly vegetated, but marshy area a little north of the airplane parts. It was here that he ran into Lieutenant David Cox, Corporal Jack Anderson, and PFC James Schmidt. Within moments after the four Marines came together PFC Schmidt was shot in the jaw by what may very well have been a stray bullet. Corporal Anderson quickly knelt down and picked up PFC Schmidt and put him into a fireman's carry as the four Marines moved out of their current location. Not exactly sure where they were going, the four headed through the heavy cover in a southwesterly direction which brought them to the security of the Fourth Battalion, 10th Marines.[8]

    PFC Carl Leonhardt remembered that crazy morning of July 7th. Even as the men on gun 3 were busy blasting round after round into the oncoming attackers, the magnitude of the attack caused Leonhardt to be concerned that he, "... would never see home again since we were losing so many men in the initial attack." While still firing the howitzer Leonhardt was hit in the shoulder, but the wound was not severe enough

---

[8] Ralph Mills, Interview with author, August 3, 1990, Dubuque, Iowa.

to prevent him from continuing to do his part. He recalled that the Japanese fire was thick enough that the small howitzer gunsight was hit; not that losing the gunsight was a problem since, at the time, the procedure being used was to just point the tube and fire since there were plenty of targets everywhere. When the word was given to abandon the guns and fall back, Leonhardt grabbed his carbine and started to back away from the gunline. Unlike many others who did not know for sure where they were going as they crossed the road behind the gunline, Leonhardt had scouted the area the previous evening and therefore knew where a large number of crates were stacked. Leonhardt knew that the crates would provide excellent cover from the attacking enemy and went there quickly.[9]

PFC Philip Spry was serving as the loader on gun 4. He had just finished ramming the 105millimeter round and canister into the breech of his section's weapon. As he spun back to receive another round to load, he was shot in the thigh and went down between the trails of the howitzer. It was very shortly after that when word was received from the XO pit to fall back off the gun line. As PFC Spry struggled to move back to the road he ran into Cpl Dogget. Dogget was returning to his old gun section after they had killed the tank with, and then abandoned, gun 1. Within moments the two were joined by PFC Holzer who managed to get back to the position from his machinegun. The three moved to the road where heavy firing down along the road prevented their immediate crossing. When an opportunity presented itself, the three Marines moved across the road as Dogget served as a crutch for the leg shot Spry. As they crossed the road and entered the trees and bushes on the other side, there was a sense of relief in getting across the open road uninjured. But, moments later a grenade landed and exploded nearby wounding both Spry and Dogget. As he regained his senses, Spry saw a large tarp covering something and crawled to it. Hoping to hide underneath the tarp he lifted up an edge and squirmed underneath. After resting for a while, Spry closely examined the object that was under the tarp with him and realized that the circular object with many protrusions was more than likely a sea mine. What it was doing two hundred yards inland he did not know, but decided that he did not want to be near it. Realizing he heard Americans talking, Spry looked out

---

[9] Carl H. Leonhardt, Interview with author, August 3, 1990, Dubuque, Iowa.

from under the tarp and saw Marines not far away behind the wing of an airplane. As he crawled to the wing the other Marines quickly grabbed him and pulled him over the wing where he lay for a while. But even though he had been twice wounded, Spry's luck went from bad to worse as a mortar round came in nearby. The explosion lifted Spry in the air and flopped him down hard. His next conscious moment came when he awoke in the bed of a hospital ship.[10]

PFC Rod Sandberg had been on duty as battery recorder all night. At just about 0400 he was relieved of his watch by PFC Swede Larson. Sandberg received instructions from Larson to help him find the foxhole that Larson had dug, which would serve as Sandberg's bed for the evening. Sandberg left the XO pit on his way to get some much-needed sleep. As he passed another man's foxhole, Sandberg was told to be quiet and be still as there were Japanese on the road behind the gunline. As he took a hard look in the darkness at the road, Sandberg could hardly believe his eyes when he observed not only Japanese soldiers, but enemy tanks as well. Sandberg returned to the XO pit to tell Lieutenant Hofstetter what he had seen. It was about this time that the battery first observed the large wave of Japanese soldiers moving toward them. As the gunline opened fire on the advancing enemy to their front, Sandberg moved to gun 2 in order to assist with the firing. Round after round was fired at the Japanese, but they just kept coming. To Sandberg it appeared that the Japanese were low crawling toward the Marines and at a certain point would get up and rush toward the gunline. In the early morning hours, he could not see that the Japanese were coming up out of the little streambed. Sandberg noticed that the howitzer section chief, Corporal Leonard Froncek, was on the ground having been shot in the foot. He bent down to assist Froncek to get his boot off. As the two men worked to undo the knots of Froncek's boot word was received that the men were to fall back as the gunline had become untenable. Sandberg could not locate his rifle as he started to leave the gunline; he did notice, however, that Corporal Froncek was still on the ground. Approaching the wounded Marine, Sandberg said he had no rifle as someone else must have picked it up so he would assist the corporal. For reasons unknown, Froncek would not hear of it and ordered the PFC

---

[10] Philip Spry, Interview with author, September 11, 1992, Dubuque, Iowa.

to take the corporals weapon and fall back. Obeying orders Sandberg moved toward the road behind the gunline.[11]

PFC Henry Basford had been with an artillery FO team in support of the action on Mt Tapotchau. He rejoined How Battery and the 3d Battalion at the position east of Garapan on the 5th of July, just in time to move the following evening into the next position. Assigned to local security for the left rear of the H position, PFC Basford and two other Marines dug a foxhole in a clearing in the brush to occupy as their position. A shelter half was erected by the Marines to keep any rain off them that might come down that evening. It was still very early in the morning when Basford observed, "Nine or ten Japanese came into the clearing. They were real close before we realized that they were Japanese, for it was just getting light and we really weren't expecting Japanese." The three Marines opened fire on the group of Japanese soldiers in the clearing. Quickly the Japanese set up an automatic weapon they had with them and returned fire on the Marines. In addition, the attackers began to throw grenades at the Marines in the foxhole. Basford was quick enough to deftly throw back the first two grenades, but as the third grenade rolled into the fighting hole it kept going until it was back under the rear of the erected shelter half. As Basford groped for the grenade, he grabbed it with his hand as the grenade exploded. Basford's hand disintegrated when the grenade exploded, but it absorbed enough of the explosion for all three Marines to keep fighting since the other two suffered only minor wounds and Basford was still able to assist with only one hand. Basford's wound was cauterized and not bleeding much. Within a short time, the Marines knew that there were many more Japanese in the area than the initial nine or ten they encountered. As they considered the tactical situation and the severe wound of Basford's hand, the three men started to withdraw from their position toward the gunline where they hoped to find a corpsman and the security of numbers. When the three Marines arrived at the gunline they immediately realized that the battery was falling back. Basford also started moving back from the rear of the gunline. Basford's wrist started to bleed heavily as he dove into the bushes on the other side of the road.[12] In the

---

[11] Rod Sandberg, "Battery "O" 5th Bn." (Sic.), Date unknown, Bixby, Oklahoma, p. 13.
[12] Henry R. Basford, Letter to author, Date unknown, Paonia, Colorado.

same area was Les Hobach who realized that Basford could not last long with his wrist in that condition. Hobach took his web belt off and wrapped it around Basfords lower forearm. Using his Kabar knife for leverage Hobach tightened the tourniquet to stop the bleeding. The two then continued their hunt for a better location.[13]

As the How Battery Marines withdrew to their rear, they ran, hobbled, crawled, and were carried through the brush and trees behind the gunline. At about 20 yards they reached the road. To their dismay, getting across the road was easier said than done as machine gun fire from an enemy tank threatened anyone who tried to cross. The firing MG was not scattering rounds everywhere, but seemed to have a methodical pattern of always starting on the same side of the road and then shifting to the other side as he fired. In addition, the height of the path of the machine gun fire was noticed to be high enough that a low rolling crossing of the road increased one's chances of making it. One of the Marines who noticed this was PFC Paul M. Sarvageau. As some of the Marines approached the road near Sarvageaus location he stopped them to give advice about the tanks pattern of firing along the road. Then PFC Sarvageau functioned as a starter by telling his fellow Marines when to start across and to hit the ground and roll quickly into the undergrowth and safety of the opposite side.[14]

The order to abandon the gunline had originated from the XO pit located just behind gun 2. At Captain Nelson's order, Lieutenant Hostetter passed the word to the men, and then those in the area of the XO pit started to move to the rear of the position themselves. Lieutenant Hal Lanes last glance past the gunline saw the attackers still coming, "...waving rifles over their heads, yelling and screaming." As he turned and started to move to the rear, Lieutenant Lane came upon the lifeless body of PFC Donald Irwin who had been in Lanes FO team up on Mt Tapotchau. The lieutenant could not fight off the intense sorrow he felt to see his friend lying there shot in the head. For a moment he almost fell victim to panic, but then maintained his composure and continued his retreat to find a safer location. A few seconds later Lane met with PFC Everett Hinton and the two arrived

---

[13] Lester Hobach tape.
[14] Rod Sandberg, Interview with author, September 11, 1992, Dubuque, Iowa.

at the road and quickly crossed. On the other side of the road, they entered into another partly wooded and partly brushy area. Within about 30 yards they came upon a likely rampart that was provided by what appeared to be an aviation parts supply area.[15]

A good number of other Marines from the battery also came upon this area where a large number of crates and airplane wings were lying about. This might be the best place the Marines could find to make a stand and they had to do so quickly as the Japanese pressed their attack. As best they could, the men assembled the crates and whatever was at hand to create a protective barrier from which they could defend themselves.[16]

---

[15] Harold A. Lane, "Recollections of the 10th Marines," March, 1990, Santa Rosa, California, p. 15.

[16] Multiple interviews with members of H Battery, September 11, 1992, Dubuque, Iowa.

Chapter 14

H & S Battery sent only a forward command post to the position it occupied the night of 6 July. Its position, just across the road and a little southeast of How Battery, was hit within a very short time of the attack on How Battery. The layout of the battalion forward command post (CP) consisted of one tent that served as the battalion Fire Direction Center (FDC) and communication center, as well as a second tent nearby that was the Battalion Aid Station (BAS). A third tent the men erected was a tarp in which to stow their gear and sleep under. The tents were erected on a wooded levee that branched off from the road in a southwesterly direction as the road went south. The tents sat among some trees and tall grass on the levee. To the north and northwest the trees and scrub growth were thicker. To the west and south of the battalion CP the terrain was mostly open fields that had been tilled, in the past, but at that time had no crops cultivated. The same was true of the area immediately to the east.[1]

Captain Young was assigned, by Major Crouch, to serve as a liaison officer to the 4th Battalion while the two battalions were formed into the artillery group in support of the 4th Marine Division. Young was at the 4/10 position that morning, but in constant communication with 3/10 by means of a landline established over the 1000 yards that separated the two units. It was very early in the morning when Young heard some intensified firing much closer than what they had been hearing previously. Young called Major Crouch to inquire about the situation. At that time, Crouch told Young that they too heard the intensified firing to the front, but there was no firing in the area around the battalion command post and no enemy to be seen. However, it was obvious that something was not right so the two officers agreed to keep in continuous communication. As

---

[1] Dodd Sellers, "As I Recall: Remembering 1941-1946," March 12, 1991, Tuscaloosa, Alabama. p. 43.

a result of the location and intensity of the firing, the battalion commander felt much anxiety when he did not hear from How Battery. It was obvious that there was a hell of a fight going on there. Then word came in from Item Battery that they had Japanese advancing on them and were taking them under fire. Only a short while after that, Major Crouch called Captain Young to report that a Japanese tank was on the road near the Battalion FDC tent. Immediately after that the landline communication was broken and it became necessary to turn on and establish contact with the SCR-300 radio. Once communication was reestablished, Crouch instructed Young to attempt to get help from nearby army units if possible. Then he told Young to try and get a bazooka and bring it forward to the 3/10 location.

The battalion S-2 was able to get a bazooka and four rockets. Then he and two others started northeast along the coast road to get to the H&S Battery forward position. On the road they spotted two Army tanks and were surprised to see the Third Battalion surgeon, Dr. Zinberg, talking to the tankers. The tanks were unable to leave their location, to help 3/10 as the doctor requested, without authority from Army superiors. Unable to get help from the tanks, Captain Young, Lieutenant Commander Zinberg, and the two other men started to cross the open field to the west of the H&S position. Before they got moving, Captain Allan Tully arrived at their location. He too was attempting to get the assistance of the tanks. Tully said he would show Young the best vantage point from which to fire on the tank if it was still in the same location. As they moved to the east across the open field, the five were taken under fire by a machinegun from the northwest corner of the field and Captain Tully was hit. As Doctor Zinberg assisted Tully, the wounded captain instructed the impromptu bazooka team where to go to fire on the tank. Tully was very fortunate that the Japanese bullet that hit him did so at such an angle that it penetrated the skin on his right side and then ricocheted off a rib and immediately exited out again. As the impromptu bazooka team arrived at the tree line, they met with some of the men who were part of the H&S communication and fire direction sections. Looking out the other side of the tree line, Young could clearly see the tank at what he judged to be close to 100 yards to the northeast. Unfortunately, all four of the bazooka rounds fired at the Japanese tank missed their mark. Young sent a man back to get more rockets for the bazooka, and proceeded to assess the situation.[2]

PFCs Dodd Sellers and Sam Ridley were awake to stand the 0400 watch in the CP tent. Sellers was a radio operator and Ridley was a computer-man from the instrument section that figured the firing data within the FDC. After assuming their watch, the two Marines stood together looking at the situation map to determine if there had been any significant changes during the night. After being satisfied with what he saw on the map, Sellers turned away to sit down and conduct a radio check with the battalion rear CP, still at the previous position. Suddenly there was a loud noise. The tank that was on the road between How and H & S had fired into the CP tent where Sellers and Ridley were located. The round or fragmentation ripped a large hole in the side of the tent and hit Ridley on the upper back and right shoulder. Fortunately, it did not explode, but hit Ridley with a glancing impact that knocked him down and continued out through the other side of the tent. As Sellers remembers, "Through the opening in the tent I saw a Japanese tank on the road with its gun pointing at the tent. Instinctively I hit the deck because I was sure it would fire again..." However, the tank came under fire as How Battery gun 4 fired several 105millimeter rounds into it. Although he had no way of determining what the source of fire on the enemy tank was, Sellers recalled seeing smoke coming out of the tank hatch. This provided him an opportunity to check on Ridley who was found alive on the ground near the entrance of the tent. Immediate first aid consisted of sprinkling sulfa powder from both their first aid kits on the exposed wounds and making Ridley as comfortable as possible. After he finished tending to Ridley, Sellers decided to go to the aid station for help. As he moved from within the canvas of the CP tent toward the BAS, Sellers was appalled to witness the large number of Marines and Corpsman lying dead around it. In need of a weapon for himself, Sellers took a carbine from a dead Marine but then realized the man had no rounds of ammo left to use in it. As he moved back to the CP tent, Sellers discovered that the battalion radio was still functional so he sent a quick call to the battalion rear advising them of the situation. He spoke with PFC Frank Horne and warned the rear of how

---

[2] Gavin Young, Personal account of Japanese attack written the day after the attack, 1992, Dubuque, Iowa.

precarious the situation was. He then recommended that it was not wise to attempt a rescue since there were Japanese everywhere and chances of getting through would be slim. While Sellers' advice was well-intended, it was wasted words as Marines at the rear echelon positions were already reacting to help their fellow Marines in trouble.[3]

Corporal Anthony Kouma was a member of H & S Battery machinegun section. He arrived at the position late as a result of a flat tire on the truck he was riding in. After becoming familiarized with several shell holes used as outposts, Corporal Kouma was assigned to take charge of local security on the eastern side of H&S Battery position. After verifying the placement of all security posts, he set up a mosquito net and settled in for the night. Before light next morning, Corporal Kouma was notified of some activity to the front. As he grabbed his carbine and helmet, Kouma headed out to check with the Marines manning the outposts. It seems that two Americans were seen hurriedly moving back through the H & S position on their way to the rear. When they would not even stop to answer questions, it aroused the suspicion of the Marine sentries. Shortly after Corporal Kouma arrived at the outposts, it was beginning to get light out. Hearing a noise to his left the Corporal turned to see a single Japanese taking aim at him. Three quick shots from the carbine fired by Kouma killed the lone Japanese. It was not long after that when the Marines saw a tank moving south down the road. As the tank stopped near the CP tent a lone figure emerged from the turret. Without thinking Kouma fired a quick shot at the figure and then cursed himself for shooting because he thought he might have shot at an American tanker. It was still dark enough that at a distance it was very difficult to determine who and what things really were. But the darkness may have worked to the Americans' advantage because as it turned lighter, the firing coming from Japanese soldiers intensified. Corporal Kouma fought with and directed the fire of PFC's Oldenburger, Connery, Jenkens and Spencer as the five Marines repulsed the Japanese attack in their area. With a BAR (Browning Automatic Rifle) and carbines, they fought against devastating Japanese machine gunfire. As Spencer was hit and went down, they tore open his shirt to see how bad it was. At first glance Kouma believed

---

[3] Sellers, "As I Recall," pp. 44,45.

Spencer was gut shot, but then realized the blood was originating from the shoulder and running down across Spencer's chest and accumulating on his stomach and in his navel. After quickly treating their wounded comrade, Oldenburger and Kouma continued to fire on the Japanese machine gun giving them so much trouble. For some reason during the firefight with the machine gun Kouma remembered that it was Oldenburger's birthday and yelled Happy Birthday to him. The return remark to Kouma said something about a son-of-a-bitch. Although they were successful in keeping the Japanese out of their position it became obvious that a shortage of ammo would soon make that impossible. When the decision was made to move from their fighting holes into the thicker vegetation, the Marines moved and covered each other. As he carried Spencer, who was oblivious to the fighting as a result of the medicine they gave him, Corporal Kouma reached the heavily vegetated area. But, Jenkens was killed as he dashed out of his fighting hole. As the fighting continued, Kouma moved around the area and assessed the situation. A stroke of luck brought Kouma together with Corporal Bailey Nabers, who was carrying a light .30 caliber machine gun. The good fortune was that he met Nabers just before coming upon a deep drainage ditch with many Japanese moving through it. By the time Kouma stopped firing the BAR and Nabers stopped firing the .30 caliber machine gun, the ditch was full of dead Japanese. However, the real danger of receiving incoming mortar rounds began so the Marines hit the deck and were lucky to escape with a couple of perforated ear drums. As they moved southward along the road the Marines met up with Army forces. After getting a resupply of ammo the two started back to help their friends still at the H&S position.[4]

At the CP tent no Japanese attempted to occupy the tent for several hours. However, later that morning Sellers and Ridley were joined by PFCs Lester Coop, Pappy Bruce, and a third Marine they did not know. With the benefit of five men, they were able to organize a better defense of the tent with a Marine manning each corner of the tent from which to watch for Japanese still aggressively prowling through the area. All along the base of the tent there was a wall of sandbags about three or four sandbags high. These small barriers often served more to keep rain water

---

[4] Anthony Kouma, Letter to author, June 13, 1990, Encinitis, California.

from running into the tent than to protect the men inside; however, on this morning it was all the protection the Marines had and they stayed low and close to the sandbags the best they could. Throughout the remainder of the morning Sellers, Coop and Bruce all received gunshot wounds as bullets often peppered the tent, but they held out. Possibly because the Japanese did not know how few Marines were in the tent, they never rushed the CP. However, when the Marines in the tent saw the mortar rounds impacting closer and closer toward them it was obvious that something had to be done fast. They decided their chances against Japanese bullets as they ran were better than their chances against a Japanese mortar as they lay there. The decision was made by all to carry Ridley out as they made a run for it. Sellers was covered by the others as he quickly crawled toward the aid station and retrieved a stretcher on which to carry Ridley. Even though he was in great pain and his right arm hung uselessly limp, Ridley insisted that his legs were okay and that he would run with the others as he did not want to slow them down by carrying him. On the command "Go" the five Marines took off on a sprint for their lives. They ran in a southwesterly direction through the open field toward a drainage ditch that would provide cover in the direction of friendly forces. Sporadic rifle fire was fired at the fleeing Marines and just as they reached the ditch a machinegun opened up also. The MG was too late as the five men jump into the concrete lined ditch and into safety from the Japanese fire.[5]

    By this time Captain Young realized that most of the men who were still alive and in the HQ area had gravitated together and were in small pockets of resistance. The two largest groups were in the tree line but separated by a distance of approximately 80 yards. One group, including Major Crouch, was in a protected area close to the tents while the other group was further south in the tree line. The group to the south received a small resupply of much needed ammo. The men located nearer the tents were taking some heavy fire from the Japanese attackers so Lieutenant Hoyt Stewart started forward along the tree line with some men to try and assist in taking off some of the pressure the others were receiving. After about 50 yards, the would-be relief party also came under very heavy fire and was pinned down. Still determined to get through to

---

[5] Sellers, "As I Recall," pp. 45-48.

the beleaguered men, Captain Young and a few others started forward to assist Stewart and the others as they attempted to reach the FDC area where the battalion commander and a few others were still holding out. As Young reached Stewart's position, Lieutenant Stewart was seriously wounded. Young knew that Stewart would need the attention of Dr. Zinberg, so the captain started back to where he had just been. Arriving there, Captain Young discovered the doctor with the fatally wounded Lieutenant Charles Hight. Being unable to do anything more for Hight, the doctor moved forward to assist with Stewart. Patching up Stewart the best he could was not going to be enough, so the doctor ordered Stewart taken back to better care if he was to have any hope of surviving. Unfortunately, the lieutenant died before he could be moved.

A little later Captain Young was able to get to the forward area and link up with Major Crouch. Since Young was able to get forward, it might be possible for the wounded to get back so the CO went to round up all he could in order to send them out with the captain.[6]

Corporal Claude Corbin and Mess Sergeant Alfred P. Jensen were sleeping in adjacent foxholes in the open field about 30 yards west of the H&S CP tent. It was not yet light when, according to Corbin, both Marines were, "...awakened to close firing." Being unable to see what was happening they grabbed their carbines and started to roll toward the CP tent. Before they could get to the tent, Corbin looked up toward the road and saw the outline of a Japanese tank with troops on it. As he fired into the Japanese he glanced to his left and saw the battalion communication chief, Staff Sergeant Lea Bell, also firing on the enemy soldiers from a position under a jeep. The Japanese soldiers dispersed and Corbin continued to look around the area. To the north he heard much shooting and yelling coming from where he thought How Battery was located. As he was looking in that direction Corbin suddenly observed many Japanese coming out of the heavy foliage. With only his carbine for firepower, he started shooting the oncoming enemy attackers. As he heard another weapon open fire on the Japanese, Corbin saw that his fire was being augmented by the heavier fire of Bailey Nabers' .30 caliber machinegun. Not one Japanese escaped their accurate and deadly fire. Firing was now

---

[6] Young, Personal account.

heard from many different locations as Corbin made his way to the tent on the wooded levee. In the immediate area around the tent were many dead and wounded. Corbin then heard a voice he recognized and turned to see another Marine attempting to crawl for help with a wounded leg. Corbin and Corpsman Yeager went to help the wounded Marine. After the corpsman bandaged the gunshot wound, Corbin assisted his buddy in getting away from the area going through the trees to a ditch that provided cover for the men to get back to friendly lines. From that location where the tree line and drainage ditch came together, Corbin also saw the two Army tanks on the road by the coast. Traveling in the ditch he arrived at the road and went to the location of the tanks to ask them if they would follow him to H&S Battery in order to help relieve the unit. After the tanks informed him that they could not leave their position without orders from their higher headquarters, Corbin started back to H&S by himself. Along the way he ran into the NCOIC of the machinegun section, Sergeant Kenneth Sartin. After hearing the story, the sergeant told Corbin to continue toward the CP to tell an officer about the Army tanks. Near the tent he found the battalion intel officer. Captain Young already knew about the tanks and he instructed Corbin to go to the tent and tell the battalion commander about them. As Corbin entered the shredded piece of canvas that was once a tent, he saw Major Crouch approach him. Because it was safer, and because he was exhausted, Corbin flopped to the ground and began to tell the battalion commander about the location of the two tanks and what they told him. Before Corbin had a chance to say anything else the major quickly exited the tent through the large hole in the side. It was obvious by the way he left that Major Crouch wanted those tanks in a bad way. Corbin wanted to advise the major on the safest way to travel to the tanks but the CO departed so quickly he was unable to do so.[7]

  Major Crouch was very anxious to have the two Army tanks assist his unit since he knew there was still a Japanese tank in the area. With this in mind, he decided to go himself to seek help from the tanks. The battalion commander instructed Captain Young to provide a Marine to go with him and to take charge of the area while he was gone. More concerned about the precarious situation his beleaguered men were in than his own personal

---

[7] Claude Corbin, Letter to author, May 31, 1991, Bloomfield, Indiana.

safety, he did not take the time to travel the longer but safer way. Instead, Major Crouch traveled across the open field which was the shortest distance to the tanks. The distance was about 150 yards that he would have to travel; however, he was hit by Japanese fire at about the halfway point. As he flinched from his wound his helmet came off and he dropped his carbine. Seriously wounded the courageous major continued another 20 yards before his wound dropped him to the ground. Knowing that he had very little time left to live Major Crouch's thoughts turned to his loved ones back home and he was able to get a couple of letters from his pocket to read one last time. Whether or not he was ever able to read these letters one last time will never be known as Major Crouch died of his wounds while holding them.[8]

Pharmacist Mate Frederick Barrows of Ness City, Kansas was in H&S Battery and the senior corpsman of 3/10. As the fighting continued and the casualties mounted, it became obvious that there were many more casualties than he could treat. But that did not deter Barrows from trying even when it meant exposing himself to the deadly fire of Japanese weapons. As Barrows moved around the battlefield attending to the wounded, he received a serious wound in the shoulder. While in a hole with two other Marines Barrows saw another corpsman he did not know join them in their protective position. Robert Pyle was a corpsman with King Battery of Fourth Battalion, Tenth Marines. Although 4/10 was located almost 1000 yards behind the 3/10's position, when the fight was going on Pyle moved forward to see if he could determine what was happening. When Pyle got close enough, he could see across an open field what appeared to be several wounded Marines in a hole. Pyle moved forward to assist the injured men and was shot in the arm himself before arriving at the hole they occupied. As Pyle noticed the severity of the wound that Barrows had sustained to his shoulder, the 4/10 corpsman applied a dressing to his fellow sailor. According to Pyle it was only a very short time after he treated Barrows wound that the cry for a corpsman was heard. Almost as if he were on automatic, Barrows got up out of the hole to start toward the call for assistance. Just as he got out of the hole a mortar round exploded knocking the senior 3/10 corpsman back in the hole.

---

[8] Robert Sherrod, On to Westward, (New York: Duell, Sloan, & Pearce 1945). p. 137.

Fragmentation from the mortar round also hit and seriously wounded Pyle, who then started back toward the 4/10 position with the two wounded Marines. Barrows, however, went again toward the calls for help. It was not long until Pharmacist Mate Barrows discovered that he did not have the strength to keep going. With seven different wounds in his body, he lay there on his back in an open field looking up at the sun, expecting to die. After losing consciousness he came around to find himself on a hospital ship.[9]

Pyle was not the only man from the 4th Bn to come to the aid of 3d Bn that day. One of the others was PFC Harold Agerholm of Racine, Wisconsin. After learning of the fighting going on ahead of their position, Agerholm asked for and was granted permission to go forward to attempt to assist as he was able. He took an unused jeep ambulance sitting nearby and drove toward the sound of the fierce fighting ahead of him. Agerholm did not have far to travel before he found wounded Marines in need of assistance. Some were making their own way south while others he came upon would probably not have made it much further[10] if Agerholm had not put them in the jeep ambulance and evacuated them to safety. During the course of several hours the courageous PFC made repeated trips into the perilous environment to assist his wounded comrades. Single-handedly at times, and often braving heavy rifle and mortar fire, PFC Agerholm loaded and evacuated the wounded Marines he could find. Though he had rescued approximately 45 casualties already, when he saw what appeared to be two wounded Marines, PFC Agerholm again braved enemy fire to go to their assistance. In his attempt to do so, the heroic young Marine was shot and killed by a Japanese sniper. For his actions, PFC Harold Agerholm was posthumously awarded the Medal of Honor.[11]

When the Japanese attack hit the forward battalion position, things at the rear position were quiet and uneventful. Lieutenant Buss was resting peacefully and wearing a set of headphones as he monitored the radio net to the forward position. Suddenly the radio was receiving loud frantic calls that the Japanese had overrun the forward position. Moments later Buss

---

[9] Robert Pyle, Letter to author, April 6, 1992, Blaine, Minnesota.
[10] Mrs. Frederick Barrows, Letter to author, May 13, 1992, Pueblo, Colorado.
[11] Harold Agerholm, Medal of Honor citation.

recognized the voice of Major Crouch on the radio. The battalion commander instructed his communication officer to call regiment and division and let them know what was happening. As Lieutenant Buss remembers that conversation, he noted that Major Crouch sounded, "...quite calm and matter-of-fact."[12]

---

[12] Wilbur Buss, Letter to author, May 18, 1990, Lake Elsinore, California.

Chapter 15

As the Japanese continued their attack to the southwest over the Tanapag Plain, the Japanese forces on the left flank of the attack turned toward the south and in the direction of the Marines of Item Battery. The Item Position was south-southeast of How's position and about 250 yards away. The guns were positioned just below the intersection of the Tanapag Plain railroad track and the road that How and H&S Batteries used to get into their locations. The railroad track ran from the Northeast to the Southwest and was built upon a berm which obscured much of Item's view of the plain to the Northwest. This did not concern most of the Marines in Item Battery since they knew that How Battery was to their left. Item also believed that the Japanese were defeated.[1]

PFC Tony Zito and the rest of his duty section just assumed the watch on their howitzer about a half hour earlier that morning when "all hell broke loose" to the north of them. As the Marines speculated about what might be going on, word finally came down that a massive Japanese attack was underway and it appeared that How Battery had been hit really hard and possibly overrun. Details of exactly what was going on were very sketchy, but a runner from How was supposedly on his way to Item to provide a status report. Lieutenant Paul Roeder, XO of Item Battery, told Zito to go up the road a short way in order to receive the runner and to make sure that he was from How and not the Japanese army. Zito moved on the road a little way and waited; soon he saw his expected messenger. To be sure that the approaching figure was who he should be, Zito challenged him with a big booming voice that halted the man in his tracks. The next thing heard was the messenger saying, "Zito, is that you?" Zito confirmed that it was he and told the other Marine to keep coming. The incoming Marine approached and commented, "There is only one person

---

[1] Multiple interviews with members of I Battery, September 11, 1992, Dubuque, Iowa.

with a voice like that!" Just as the two men arrived back in the Item position the battery started to receive small arms fire from the approaching Japanese. Zito did the same as the rest of the Marines in Item Battery who were taking cover the best they could behind their howitzers, or whatever terrain provided an advantageous position to protect them from the fire of the attacking Japanese. Lying on the ground they fired their carbines at the assaulting enemy force, but before too much time passed the men found themselves running short of ammo. As he discovered that he was about to run out of ammo, Zito again took advantage of his loud thunderous voice to call for more ammo to fire from his carbine. Moving back and forth between the men with some more ammo was Sergeant Keith Neal. As the senior sergeant heard Zito's call for ammo he threw a full clip at Zito. Even though he had called for ammo, Zito's mind was very much still on firing at the enemy with the little ammo he had remaining. When he felt the sharp jab of the thrown ammo clip hit him in the back, it so startled Zito initially that it made him think that he had been hit by some type of enemy fire. A quick loud scream made Zito's fears known to all. Then he realized what really happened and that his scream was uncalled for since he had not really been hit. For a short while after that Zito seemed to forget about the Japanese and everything else except cussing out Neal for scaring him so.[2]

The night of 6 July, after the position was fairly well established, PFC Robert Olson and PFC Jack Wood laid out their bedrolls and set up mosquito nets over them in order to get a good night's sleep. These two Marines were the BAR team on gun 4, and laid down in front of their howitzer, which was located to the left of the battery position and adjacent to the railroad berm. As Olson remembers 7 July, "Sometime around 0230 there was sporadic gunfire around us and toward Marpi Point." Word had also gotten around that a battery machinegun had killed a Japanese infiltrator and there was speculation of a possible attack. Later that morning speculation became reality as Olson and Wood were awakened by the sound of gunfire. Bullets and some tracers were whining around the two Marines. A couple of bullets even pierced the mosquito netting that hung over them. Olson and Wood scurried quickly back behind their

---

[2] Anthony Zito, Letter to author, December 1, 1990, Forrest Hills, Pennsylvania.

howitzer to the protection it provided. After scrutinizing the situation, they decided to help the machinegun team set up just to the left of their position. The machinegun, manned by PFC's Edward L. Philips and Donald B. Evans, was set up on the railroad berm which gave them a good field of fire on the plain on the other side. However, as some of the Japanese were able to get in close enough to the bottom of the steep berm, the Marines machinegun was not able to depress enough to shoot them. The other side of the coin was that the Japanese could not shoot the Marines either; but now the Japanese were within hand grenade range of the machinegun nest. As the Japanese threw the first grenades at the Marines it is very likely that they were totally surprised by the Yankee ingenuity they came up against. As the grenades were thrown at Philips and Evans, a loud clanging noise sent the grenades right back at the attackers. Olson looked over and saw Evans holding a piece of sheet metal that Evans was using to bat away any grenade that came close to him and Philips and their machinegun.

It was obvious that the standoff could not go on much longer and Olson and Wood realized that they could shoot the Japanese better by being on the other side of the berm. Moving Southwest along the railroad tracks, the two Marines came to the culvert under the railroad tracks and through the berm where a drainage ditch ran. As they went through the culvert and came out the other side, Olson and Wood could look to the Northeast along the berm and have a clear field of fire at many Japanese soldiers. As the two were taking the Japanese under fire from their new position along the drainage ditch, they were joined by a handful of other men from Item Battery. The Marines in the ditch were taking their toll on the attacking enemy but soon found themselves running short of ammo. With only a couple of rounds left in his clip, Olson decided he must get more ammo and started moving up the ditch toward the culvert. As he did so, he was shot in the left leg and was unable to move. The shortage of ammo applied to everyone and the Japanese were still coming. Wood, PFC's Neil Taylor, George Coulter, Marion Lowe, and Edward Thompson all started back up the drainage ditch, moving and shooting and carrying Olson as they went. After the men arrived on the Southwest side of the berm and started toward the howitzers, they realized that there were now many Japanese on that side of the berm and among the howitzers. The battery had repulsed an initial onslaught, but too many Japanese and too little ammo forced them to fall back a short distance behind the gunline to a more covered position. This caused the small group of Marines who had just returned to the original battery area to continue to move to an area to the south where they could better protect themselves. It was at this area that the Marines from the nearby George Battery were able to join up with Item and help establish a solid line of defense from which to hold out against the Japanese attack.[3]

Corporal Oscar D. Sowers was one of the older Marines in Battery I, nearly forty years old. He lied about his age in order to be a Marine. It was not uncommon for the men who did not know Sowers to salute him as they approached him from a distance. Before recognizing his rank, the younger Marines assumed that this sophisticated looking gentleman was surely an officer. But on the morning of July 7th, OD Sowers was anything but sophisticated as he manned his machinegun on the Item Battery perimeter. Sowers stayed on his gun firing away at the approaching enemy even as the battery defense was being penetrated and had to fall back. Finally, the machinegun was destroyed and Sowers was severely wounded by enemy hand grenades. Then he too fell back.[4]

First Lieutenant Robert Jones was the officer in charge of the Item Battery machinegun section. As the tempo of the fighting increased and more and more Japanese continued to attack their position, several Marines on the machineguns were wounded severely enough they could no longer man their position. Knowing full well that the battery needed the heavy fire power of the machineguns, Lieutenant Jones took position behind a weapon and poured fire into the oncoming Japanese. When wounded the young officer would not abandon his post and continued to fire on the attacking enemy helping to make possible the required withdrawal to a more defensible position. Although Lieutenant Jones had not been in the battery long, he was held in high esteem by the other men as he never left his position behind the machinegun until late in the afternoon when his mortally wounded body was carried away.[5]

---

[3] Robert Olsen, Interview with author, September 11, 1992, Dubuque, Iowa.

[4] Oscar D. Sowers, Silver Star Citation and interview with members of I Battery, September 12, 1992, Dubuque, Iowa.

[5] Robert F. Jones, Silver Star Citation and interview with members of I Battery, September.

PFC George Sleutel found a .25 caliber Japanese machinegun that was a reproduction of the British made Lewis machinegun. Along with the weapon was a drum of ammo. In the morning of July 7th as the Japanese attacked their position, PFC's Sleutel, Edmund Youngbird, and Paul McNabb set up the newly acquired weapon to the front of their howitzer on a small knoll. After the Marines fired the enemy machinegun to kill the attacking Japanese, it seemed as if the other Japanese nearby recognized the sound of the Japanese weapon and incorrectly assumed that it was being fired on the Marines by one of their own. Because of this, the attacking Japanese seemed to gravitate toward the sound of the weapon, only to have Sleutel turn the machinegun on them. According to the other Marines who witnessed the results of the Marine fired Japanese machinegun, the bodies were really piled up at the bottom of the knoll that Sleutel, Youngbird, and McNabb were firing from. When their ammo ran out, the three Marines were forced to fall back also. Less than 200 yards to the rear of the gunline a small group of men came upon a large bomb crater that was to be the position from which they would hold out the remainder of the day.[6]

PFC Thomas Palmer was fighting from the cover of a foxhole by the Item gunline when a freak round landed in the hole and exploded, blowing him out of the hole. Although he was severely wounded, the corpsman rushed in to begin attending to his wounds. Due to his severe bleeding, the corpsman gave him a unit of whole blood; not long after that he was given yet another unit. When the corpsman made the decision to give him a 3rd unit of blood, Palmer refused it and told them to give it to someone to whom it would do some good. Shortly afterwards Palmer died.[7]

---

[6] Edmund Youngbird, Interview with author, August 3, 1990, Dubuque, Iowa.
[7] Multiple interviews with members of I Battery, September 12, 1992, Dubuque, Iowa.

Chapter 16

George Battery had arrived at its position very late in the afternoon of the previous day. The T in the road and the slope of the terrain required G Battery to lay all four of its howitzers on the left side of the approach road and short of the cross road. Immediately on the left side of the approach road was a large pile of very big timbers. The wooden timbers were approximately 8" X 8" X 10' in dimension, and probably positioned by the road in order to be taken at a later time to the plain below for use as railroad ties. After shifting some of the timbers away from the center of the pile, G Battery established its command post in the center of the pile of timbers and the protection they provided. George Battery was not in the ideal location to lay in a gunline as the terrain sloped downhill from gun 1 to gun 4. From this position however, the men of G Battery were able to look down on the location of Item Battery and whatever else was to their northwest.[1]

PFC James Tucker arrived in the G Battery position driving a radio jeep. A short time after arriving he was instructed to park the jeep, so he proceeded to drive the vehicle into a small group of trees. As Tucker was getting out of the jeep, he noticed a Japanese soldier lying in some nearby bushes. Taking the Japanese captive, Tucker observed him to be wounded. Closer inspection determined that the wound was infected and that gangrene had set in. Battery corpsman treated the wound as best they could before the prisoner was sent to the rear to be placed in a prisoner camp. After the prisoner left, Tucker learned he was not on the first watch. The men who were not on the first watch started to look for a place to sack out. Tucker and PFC Max Timmons were fortunate enough to grab a couple of unused stretchers to sleep on. This was a real luxury as it kept them from having to sleep on the ground still wet from the rain. Tucker

---

[1] William Zachary, Letter to author, February 12, 1992, Pomona, California.

was not exactly sure what time it was, but long before he wanted to get-up, he was awakened and told that H, I, and H&S Batteries were under attack. Tucker quickly went into the timbers CP and put on a headset to the switchboard. Just moments later he heard Major Hitt calling from regiment to ask what was going on. Tucker told the former battalion exec that apparently the other three batteries of 3/10 were under heavy attack. No sooner had he completed saying this when a battery officer arrived to speak with Major Hitt. Tucker left the CP to get his radio jeep ready to go, but received no further instructions. It was obvious to the Marines in George Battery that a lot of heavy action going on down in the lower terrain to their left, or north of the position. Most of the men began to move toward the left of the position where they faced down the hill in order to better see what was developing, and be in a better position to respond if it came their way. Tucker crossed in front of the gun line and moved out along the berm which would also face an attack toward the Item Battery position.[2]

PFC's Bill Zachary, TR Timinsky, and George Stroebel had been on duty in the battery command post until 0200 that morning. Zachary "...was awakened at approximately 0430 by distant gunfire." Moments later a stray round hit the timbers that he was lying by. Zachary woke Stroebel and the two decided to investigate what was happening. They started down the hill on the left flank of the battery position, but had not gone very far when they looked to the North and observed the Japanese force heading in their direction. Zachary and Stroebel hurried back to the battery position to report what they had seen to the battery gunny. Platoon Sergeant Michael J. Scott was awake and wondering what was going on when the two Marines arrived at his location. As Zachary and Stroebel briefed Scott about the advancing Japanese force, several other men gathered around and listened intently. Scott instructed the men to get their gear and follow him down the hill. As Scott, Zachary, and a few others moved along the road toward the Item Battery position, they encountered a large number of Japanese crossing the elevated railroad berm. The Marines quickly fired on the Japanese and killed most them, but not before PFC Stroebel was shot in the stomach. The men attempted to help

---

[2] James Tucker, Interview with author, September 12, 1992, Dubuque, Iowa.

Stroebel, but he died within a few minutes. Just moments later the Marines were surprised to see a Japanese tank cross the berm on the road they were on. As the Marines scrambled for cover, the Japanese tank cut loose with its machinegun and sprayed the area. After the tank stopped firing, Scott stood up in order to shoot at the tank, but was killed instantly when he was decapitated by a shot from the tank main gun. The tank then turned its turret toward Zachary. He observed, "The tank could not get its barrel low enough to get me in its sight. I saw the gunner's eyes and feared that it would try to crush me under its tracks, but it was probably afraid of getting in a hazardous position." Shortly after that PFC Robert Burchfield determined that his position was not as safe as he wanted it to be. As Burchfield attempted to change positions he was shot and killed by the tank machinegun. After that the tank started moving backwards along the road and crossed the railroad tracks.[3]

While this was occurring, other men from George made their way down the hill to assist the Item Marines withdraw to their secondary position. Art Davenport, Ollie Odell, and Max Timmons then set in on the upper right flank of the tied-in batteries. Because they were on the higher terrain, the G Marines were able to better observe any Japanese on the other side of the railroad track on Item's left flank. This altitude advantage also enabled the men to see farther to the north. At one point when the enemy attack was still strong, it appeared that one of the George Battery machineguns could be vulnerable to capture. Timmons exposed himself to enemy fire in order to get to the weapon. He then turned it on the enemy and fired at a cyclic rate until the weapon froze up, thereby assuring that it would not be used by the Japanese.[4]

The tank, which had backed up earlier, sat on the other side of the tracks for a while before moving forward and crossing to the George side of the tracks again. This time the tank left the road by turning west into the rolling field the road cut through. After stopping under a small group of trees the tank sprayed the area with machinegun fire. At this time the Japanese tank gunner noticed the small house located near the George Battery position. The side of the house facing up the hill was missing, but

---

[3] Zachary letter.
[4] Art Davenport, Interview with author, September 11, 1992, Dubuque, Iowa.

inside and looking down on the battle area were PFC's Dwain Erickson and Leo Mickalowski. After Mickalowski decided to move to another position, he had moved only about 50 yards, a shot from the tank main gun killed PFC Erickson who was still inside the house hoping to get a better shot at any approaching Japanese.[5] The Japanese tank continued to harass the Marines in the area below the gunline; then it made a fatal mistake. In order to get a better shot up the hill the tank positioned itself almost at the top of a little knoll. This position exposed the tanks thin bottom. PFC Edmund Sargis was manning a .50 caliber machinegun at the George position. As he observed the tank, he adjusted his fire into the tanks exposed underbelly and then cut loose with sustained fire. The burning tracer rounds caused the tank to burn and then explode. Zachary and the others, who had previously been pinned down by the tank, moved back to within their battery position.[6]

---

[5] Leo Mickalowski, Interview with author, September 11, 1992, Dubuque, Iowa.
[6] Tucker interview.

Chapter 17

Throughout the area that had been assigned to 3/10 small pockets of artillerymen were holding out the best they could against a weaker, but continuing, Japanese attack. The largest stronghold still repulsing the Japanese attack was the group of forty or so men of How Battery that had chosen a Japanese aircraft parts dump to make a stand. Less than 100 yards from their gun position the men shifted the crates around the best they could in order to establish a protective perimeter around themselves. To the east, and closest the road, were longer crates with airplane wings in them, as well as a few wings on the ground beside the crates. To the western side of the perimeter were the larger crates in the area that apparently held engines in them. Many of the crates containing engines were covered by large tarpaulins. The Marines positioned some of the smaller crates in the area on the other side of the perimeter. The contents of these crates appeared to be miscellaneous parts, but the important thing was the protection they provided. Why the Japanese forces picked this location to stage aircraft parts was a mystery since there was no runway near the area. Immediately outside the makeshift perimeter of crates, the vegetation was trees and underbrush, although the underbrush was thicker to the north as the men were able to see across an open field beyond the edge of the trees to the south. The heavy underbrush to the north created a serious problem for the defenders as it enabled the Japanese to sneak in close to the protective crates, unseen by the Marines.

From the battery area, Captain Nelson and Lieutenant Hostetter made it to the crates together. As he started to organize the defensive effort of the position, the battery commander was shot in the hip and wounded severely enough to realize he was not be able to function effectively. Captain Nelson directed that Lieutenant Hostetter take charge of the battery.[1]

At the southern end of the position were PFCs Frank Marshall and James Knibb. Although the brunt of the attack was at the other end of the position, the two men knew to not let their guard down as the Japanese were all around the position. When a Japanese dashed from one spot to another, Marshall fired a quick shot at the enemy but missed. It was no wonder that Marshall missed as that was the first time in the war that he fired his carbine. But now the two Marines knew where the Japanese was hiding so when he moved again Knibb was ready and killed the enemy soldier with one shot. As the two men continued to hold their position, Marshall's thoughts centered around hoping that they would "...see friendly folks before it got dark." He remembered reading about a unit that was surrounded for 48 hours, and Marshall hoped really hard they would not be surrounded that long.[2]

One of the strangest things that occurred during the Japanese attack was just south of the How Battery defensive position. The Japanese set up a machinegun that was oriented to fire in a southerly direction. No one could figure out why the Japanese set up the machinegun facing away from them. It may have been to fire on any reinforcements coming to the aid of 3/10, but help for the Marines did not arrive for over 9 hours. During that time the men of H Battery killed the Japanese manning the machinegun at least two times, but every time more enemy soldiers took over the machinegun, they never turned it on the Marines inside the crates of airplane parts.[3]

Shortly after arriving at the crates, Lieutenant Lane and PFC John Wollstadt were kneeling behind a crate when Wollstadt was shot. Wollstadt was drug to a more secure position, but died a few hours later. Ironically, PFC Eugene Larsen moved into that same position and was shot in the leg a short time later. As the siege against their position continued, many more Marines became casualties. PFC's Lee Gunty and Roger Nelson were wounded, but continued to man their position and fight to repulse the enemy attack. At one time, as Lieutenant Lane was moving

---

[1] Multiple interviews with members of H Battery, August 3, 1990, Dubuque, Iowa.
[2] Frank Marshall, Letter to author, date unknown, Lindsey, Oklahoma.
[3] Multiple interviews with members of H Battery.

from crate to crate to check on the status of the men, he was approaching the location of Corporal Ted Yeager. Lane wondered what was wrong as Yeager lunged at him. Yeagers action probably saved Lane's life as the corporal quickly slapped away the muzzle of a Japanese rifle that was being pointed between two crates and at Lanes head. Later that morning, three Japanese moved in close to the crates just outside of where Lieutenant Lane and Corporal William Miller were lying close to one another. Miller had a hand grenade but wasn't in a good position to throw it as a tree was in the way. Lane motioned to Miller that Miller should toss him the grenade and he would throw it at the Japanese. As the corporal tossed the grenade to Lane, the lieutenant heard the spoon pop and he realized that the grenade was live. As quick as he could, Lane flipped the live grenade at the three Japanese. It exploded as it hit the ground and killed all three of the enemy. Because the artillerymen were short of weapons and ammo, Lieutenant Lane then moved cautiously to where the dead Japanese were lying to collect their weapons: a rifle, a pistol, and a sword.[4]

    Gathering weapons from the dead enemy soldiers became the rule of the day as a result of the Marines weapon and ammo shortage. In many cases the artillerymen were forced to allow the Japanese to get in close before killing them in order to increase the chances of recovering the weapon as safely as possible.

    PFC Carl Leonhardt took a defensive position behind some of the long crates that contained the airplane wings in them. Like the other men in the position, Leonhardt and those near him were forced to conserve ammo, and therefore took turns firing at the enemy as they appeared. Several hours later in the morning, Leonhardt was joined at his position by PFC Sauvageau. Leonhardt reminded Sauvageau to be sure and stay low as the fire was very heavy at times, but just a few minutes after that Sauvageau slumped over against Leonhardt as he was shot through the front of his helmet. There was nothing else Leonhardt could do but lay the dead battery cook on the ground beside him. In addition to the Japanese small arms fire, the How Battery defenders were receiving Japanese

---

[4] Harold A. Lane, "Recollections of the 10th Marines," March, 1990, Santa Rosa, California. p. 16.

mortar fire in their position as well. In too many cases, the mortars caused casualties for the Marines, but fortunately for them, a large number of Japanese mortar rounds were duds and did not explode upon impact. Leonhardt remembered several occasions when he heard a heavy thud behind him and looked around to see the tailfin of a mortar round sticking out of the ground. However, later in the morning Leonhardt was wounded again as he was hit in the left hip by a Japanese bullet. Ironically this wound did not bother him much until he was back in the states almost 6 months later.[5]

Water was also in critically low supply. By mid-morning the wounded were especially in bad need of water. Some of the tarpaulins that covered the large crates were large enough that they were draped over the ground as well. Some of these tarpaulins caught and held water from the previous night's rain. However, there were no cups to dip out the water and many of the wounded were unable to be moved to the small amount of water in the tarps. PFC Holzer thought of the pack of cigarettes he had in his shirt pocket. The pack was open, but still had enough cigarettes in it that the pack was not crumpled. Holzer was able to slide off the bottom of the cellophane wrapper still intact. Even the seal was still holding on the bottom, so the men used the cigarette wrapper to scoop out small amounts of water to give drinks to the wounded.[6]

As the morning turned into the afternoon, it became very obvious that the battery would have to aggressively pursue getting water to drink, as well as getting reinforcements to save them. PFC Rod Sandburg knew as well as anyone that the battery situation was not good. He remembered hearing the sound of tanks on the coast road to the northwest of their defensive position. Sandburg went to the battery XO and told Lieutenant Hostetter that he would go to ask the tanks to come to their aid, assuming of course that they were American tanks. Hostetter knew very well of the danger involved in such an undertaking, and was reluctant to let Sandburg go; however, the officer knew that help was desperately needed and so he gave his consent. But first the Battery XO made sure that the courageous PFC knew that he was not being ordered to go. After Sandburg assured

---

[5] Carl Leonhardt, Interview with author, August 3, 1990, Dubuque, Iowa.
[6] Donald Holzer, Interview with author, August 3, 1990, Dubuque, Iowa.

Hostetter that wanted to go, the XO said okay. Even though ammo was in short supply, Hostetter gathered up enough rounds to make sure that Sandburg had a full clip to take with him as he set out for help. As Sandburg was leaving, he was told to take off his helmet as he approached friendly troops. That way the Americans would see his blond hair and would not mistake him for a Japanese. Sandberg told some men that he would be back with help, then he crawled out from the crates, low on his belly, just as he had been taught in boot camp. He moved toward the road they had crossed to get to the crates. As he reached the road he turned left and paralleled the road in a northerly direction toward the beach road and road junction 5. Luckily, Sandburg was able to get to the beach road, or Tanapag Road as it was formally called, without running into any Japanese. As he arrived there were four American tanks near the road junction. Although one appeared to be stalled in a shell hole off the road, the other three were in good operating condition since their engines were running smoothly as they sat there. Sandburg hurried to the closest tank and pounded on the side with the butt of his rifle. He got no response so he stepped back and fired a shot at the tank. Then he stepped back and removed his helmet as the Lieutenant had instructed. The tank turret began to move and then the hatch opened up and an American soldier appeared and asked Sandburg what he was doing. Sandburg explained the situation to the tanker and then asked if the tanks could go with him to the How Battery location to help them out. The tank commander said he would check and then disappeared down into the tank. A short time later he reappeared and said that the tanks couldn't go with Sandburg as they were ordered to proceed farther north. This was the location of the beleaguered 105th regiment. Sandburg had no choice but to return to the position where his fellow Marines were holding out. Again, luck was with Sandburg as he encountered no Japanese on his way back. After reporting to Hostetter what had transpired with the tanks, the XO asked if the tanks had at least radioed back to the rear to have some help sent their way. Sandburg replied that he did not know, but didn't think they did. Just a short time later the Marines again thought they heard the sound of tanks coming from the Tanapag Road. Again, Sandburg volunteered to go for help and was given approval to go, only this time his good fortune for avoiding Japanese was gone. As he approached RJ-5, there were several enemy soldiers near the small house across the road. Sandburg was fortunate to escape the encounter with only a slight concussion from an enemy grenade. When he arrived back at the location where the tanks had been, all he found was the stalled tank, still sitting where it had been earlier. This time he found a wounded American soldier sitting on the ground and leaning against the tank. The soldier asked Sandburg if he had any water. Sandburg said that he did not, but then he noticed a water can still strapped to the tank. Sandburg retrieved it so the two men could get a drink. Next Sandburg proceeded to climb onto, and then into the tank to find out if the radio worked. After a frustrating time of not being able to get the broken radio working, he gave up and climbed out of the tank to find a second soldier. After a brief exchange of status reports the soldier said he wanted to go with Sandburg to the battery location. Just as they started to depart the area, the other three tanks returned to that location. Again, Sandburg briefed the tank commander and then waited for the tanker to relay his report back to higher headquarters; then he started back to the battery location at the crates.[7]

While Sandburg was out of the position, Lieutenant Hostetter was forced to ask for another volunteer. The shortage of water was now critically low, and the wounded were especially in need of water to drink. In order to help alleviate this problem, Kenneth Dondero and William Miller volunteered to go for water. The two started out for the gunline area where they knew there should be several jeeps with water cans strapped to them. On the way to the former position, the two of them crawled cautiously and low to the ground. They were able to avoid any contact with the Japanese on the way to their objective. When they arrived, they discovered that every water can they found had bullet holes in it. Fortunately, none of the cans were shot through the bottom so all of the cans had at least a little water in them to provide some relief to the thirsty Marines. Now that they had some water, it would be very difficult to get the partially filled cans back to the location where the battery was holding out. Miller and Dondero decided that there was no other way to go than to

---

[7] Rod Sandberg, "Battery "O" 5th Bn." (Sic), Date unknown, Bixby, Oklahoma. pp. 17-20.

make a run for it. Although some Japanese observed the two men running to their position with the water cans in tow, none of the shots fired at them hit either of the two Marines.[8]

It wasn't long after Sandburg returned to the airplane crates and briefed Lieutenant Hostetter that a tank with some accompanying infantry arrived at the position. Some of the men were initially afraid that it was a Japanese tank they heard approaching their position. Upon realizing that it was an American tank many of them were overcome with relief. They now started to realize for the first time that they might survive. The first thing the tank did was wipe out the machinegun nest south of the Marine position that had been such a menace all day. Not long after the tanks arrival other forces arrived at the 3/10 location, to include some men from the rear position of 3/10. The surrounding area was not entirely secure as sniper fire from a wooded area was received by some of the arriving forces. Lieutenant Jim Brandt was among the newly arriving Marines from the rear position. As the sniper fire subsided, Brandt displayed more courage than good sense as he headed in the direction of the sniper to eliminate any future problems from the sniper. One shot from the sniper hit Lieutenant Brandt in the chest and killed him instantly. This was the last man killed from 3/10 that fateful day.[9] As the tank and reinforcements went to work cleaning out the remaining Japanese in the area, the pockets of surviving men began to gather together to survey the damage. There was no way to express their feelings as they struggled to accept the fact that they were still alive, yet so many of their close friends and fellow Marines were dead. How could this have happened? What went wrong? For many of the Marines in 3rd Battalion, 10th Marines the war was soon to be over. But for others there were still battles to be fought. But no matter what the future held, there was still the indisputable fact that these men fought and survived the greatest suicide attack of the war.

---

[8] William Miller & Kenneth Dondero, Interview with author, September 12, 1992, Dubuque, Iowa.
[9] Multiple interviews with members of H&S Battery, September 11, 1992, Dubuque, Iowa.

Introduction to Sources

Sources for writing this book fall under three primary categories. The first category is UNPUBLISHED SOURCES. This was the most disappointing of all sources as I found the majority of the books to be little more than a reiteration of each other. And while all the books on Saipan mentioned the disastrous Japanese suicide attack of July 7, 1944, there was nothing more than an overview in each case.

The second category consists of PUBLISHED SOURCES. This material is mostly military reports of various types, to include war diaries of the 2nd Marine Division. This material I researched from the archives of the History and Museums Division, Headquarters, United States Marine Corps, Washington, D.C., and the Washington National Records Center in Suitland, Maryland. It was this official material that I used to build the skeleton of the book.

The third category of material would serve to flesh out the skeleton. This final source was the PERSONAL INTERVIEWS AND LETTERS with the living survivors of the Saipan campaign. This book is written to describe the Saipan campaign as it was experienced by the Marines. Such a story would not be possible without the input of those Marines.

Unpublished Sources

Report on Japanese Counterattack at Saipan on morning of 7 July 1944. Commander Fifth Fleet, United States Pacific Fleet Flagship of the Commander 19 July 1944 World War II Action Reports Operational Archives Naval Historical Center Washington, D.C. Serial 00418 Box 43

Special Action Report Headquarters 10th Marines, 2nd Marine Division Fleet Marine Force, In the Field, 22 July 1944. Washington National Records Center Suitland, Maryland Accession Number 65A-4556 Box 81 Folder A21. 5-1

War Diary Headquarters Second Marine Division Fleet Marine Force In The Field January 12, 1944 Period of November 1 to December 31, 1943. Washington National Records Center Suitland, Maryland Accession Number 65A-5099 Box Number 67

War Diary Headquarters Second Marine Division Fleet Marine Force In The Field February 1, 1944 Period of January 1 to January 31, 1944. Washington National Records Center Suitland, Maryland Accession Number 65A-5099 Box Number 67

War Diary Headquarters Second Marine Division Fleet Marine Force In The Field March 1, 1944 Period of February 1 to February 29, 1944. Washington National Records Center Suitland, Maryland Accession Number 65A-5099 Box Number 67

War Diary Headquarters Second Marine Division Fleet Marine Force In The Field April 3, 1944 Period of March 1 to March 31, 1944. Washington National Records Center Suitland, Maryland Accession Number 65A-5099 Box Number 67

War Diary Headquarters Second Marine Division Fleet Marine Force In The Field May 3, 1944 Period of April 1 to April 30, 1944. Washington National Records Center Suitland, Maryland Accession Number 65A-5099 Box Number 67

War Diary Headquarters Second Marine Division Fleet Marine Force In The Field June 3, 1944 Period of May 1 to May 31, 1944. Washington National Records Center Suitland, Maryland Accession Number 65A-5099 Box Number 67

War Diary Headquarters Second Marine Division Fleet Marine Force In The Field

September 7, 1944 Period of June 1 to June 30, 1944. Washington National Records Center Suitland, Maryland Accession Number 65A-5099 Box Number 67

War Diary Headquarters Second Marine Division Fleet Marine Force In The Field September 7, 1944 Period of July 1 to July 31, 1944. Washington National Records Center Suitland, Maryland Accession Number 65A-5099 Box Number 67

Observers Report Headquarters Northern Troops and Landing Force In The Field 12 July 1944. Report by Colonel E. C. Burkhart (FA) USA. World War II Marianas Campaign Box 23 Folder 20 Archives Branch Marine Corps Research Center Marine Corps University Quantico, Virginia

G-3 Periodic Report #23 From: 1800 6 July 1944 to 1800 7 July 1944 Northern Troops and Landing Force In the Field 7 July 1944, 1800. World War II Marianas Campaign Box 25 Folder 37 Archives Branch Marine Corps Research Center Marine Corps University Quantico, Virginia

Major YOSHIDA, Kiyoshi, intelligence officer of the former 43rd Division Headquarters, special interrogation of. Headquarters Northern Troops and Landing Force, In the Field. 11 July 1944. Washington National Records Center Suitland, Maryland Accession Number 65A-4556 Box Number 86 Folder C2-3

Lieutenant General Saito's last message to Japanese officers and men defending Saipan, Confidential memo #15-44 Headquarters Northern Troops and Landing Force In the Field 12 July 1944. World War II Marianas Campaign Box 23 Folder 20 Archives Branch Marine Corps Research Center Marine Corps University Quantico, Virginia

Captured Japanese officer's personal account of "The Last Days of Lieutenant General Saito." File #5450-30-5 Headquarters Northern Troops and Landing Force In the Field 14 July 1944. Washington National Records Center Suitland, Maryland Accession Number 65A-4556 Box Number 86 Folder C2-4

Division Training Order Number 33-43 Training Directive Headquarters Second Marine Division Fleet Marine Force In The Field December 30, 1943. Washington National Records Center Suitland, Maryland Accession Number 65A-5099 Box Number 67 December War Diary Supplemental

Report of Readiness as of 29 Feb 44 Headquarters Second Marine Division Fleet Marine Force In The Field March 4, 1944. Washington National Records Center Suitland, Maryland Accession Number 65A-5099 Box Number 67 March War Diary Supplemental

Division Administrative Order Number. . .27:Control Of Individual Equipment Headquarters Second Marine Division Fleet Marine Force In The Field 28 March 1944. Washington National Records Center Suitland, Maryland Accession Number 65A-5099 Box Number 67 March War Diary Supplemental

Division Training Memorandum Number. . .42-44: Aerial Observer School Second Marine Division Fleet Marine Force In The Field March 4, 1944. Washington National Records Center Suitland, Maryland Accession Number 65A-5099 Box Number 67 April War Diary Supplemental

Division Training Memorandum Number. . .79-44: Parade Second Marine Division Fleet Marine Force In The Field April 9, 1944.
Washington National Records Center Suitland, Maryland Accession Number 65A-5099 Box Number 67 April War Diary Supplemental

4th Marine Division Operations Report 15 June - 9 July 1944 World War II Marianas Campaign Box 35 Folder 76 Archives Branch Marine Corps Research Center Marine Corps University Quantico, Virginia

Northern Troops and Landing Force Headquarters Operation Plan 3-44 1 May 1944 World War II Marianas Campaign Box 25 Folder 20 Archives Branch Marine Corps Research Center Marine Corps University Quantico, Virginia

Commander Joint Expeditionary Force Marianas (Task Force 51) Report of Amphibious Operations for the Capture of the Marianas Islands (Forager Operation) 25 August 1944 World War II Reports COMPHIBSPAC Operational Archives Naval Historical Center Washington, D.C. Serial 00704 Box 553

Published Sources

Costello, John. *The Pacific War.* New York: Rawon, Wade, 1981.

Crowl, Philip A. *U.S. Army in World War II, The War in the Pacific-Campaign in the Marianas.* Washington: Office of the Chief of Military History, Department of the Army, 1960.

Dyer, George Carrol. *The Amphibians Came to Conquer: The Story of Admiral Richard Kelly Turner, Volume II.* Washington: U.S. Government Printing Office, 1969.

Gabaldon, Guy. *Saipan: Suicide Island.* Saipan: Gabaldon, 1990.

Hoffman, Carl W. *The Beginning of the End.* Washington: Historical Division, Headquarters, United States Marine Corps, 1950.

Hoyt, Edwin P. *To The Marianas.* New York: Van Nostrand Reinhold, 1980.

Johnston, Richard W. *Follow Me! The Story of the 2nd Marine Division in World War II.* New York: Random House, 1978.

Jones, C. Don. *Oba, The Last Samurai - Saipan 1944-45.* Novato, California: Presidio Press, 1986.

Love, Edmund G. *The 27th Infantry Division in World War II.* Washington: Infantry Journal Press, 1949.

Millett, Allan R. *Semper Fidelis-The History of the United States Marine Corps.* New York: Macmillan, 1980.

Opotowsky, Stanford, Sergeant, USMC, Combat Correspondent, *We're All Infantrymen.* Leatherneck, January, 1945.

Pratt, Fletcher. *The Marines War.* New York: William Sloane, 1948.

Russ, Martin. *Line of Departure: Tarawa.* Garden City, New York: Doubleday, 1975.

Shaw, Henry I., Jr. and Bernard C. Nalty and Edwin C. Turnbladh. *Central Pacific Drive-History of U.S. Marine Corps Operations in World War II, Volume III.* Washington: Historical Branch, G-3 Division, Headquarters, U.S. Marine Corps, 1966.

Sherrod, Robert. *On to Westward.* New York: Duell, Sloan, & Pearce, 1945.

Singer, Kurt. *Mirror, Sword, & Jewel.* London: Croom Helm, 1973.

Smith & Pelz. *Shoulder Sleeve Insignia of the U.S. Armed Forces 1941-1945.* Erin, Tennessee: R.W. Smith, 1981.

Spector, Ronald H. *Eagle Against the Sun.* New York: Free Press, 1985.

Stockman, James R., Captain, USMC. *The Taking of MT. TAPOTCHAU.* Marine Corps Gazette, July, 1946.

Personal Interviews and Letters

The following former Marines provided me with valuable information and insight to the Saipan campaign and the July 7th suicide attack. By way of letters, tapes, drawings, maps, old papers, interviews, and listening to them reminisce, I was able to learn a wealth of information. Although not every name listed is specifically quoted in the end notes, all contributed to my education for writing this book.

Hugh Adams   Joplin, Missouri

James Appleyard   Saratoga, California

Walter Bakula   Miller Falls, Massachusetts

Allen Ball   Bakersfield, California

Jean Barrows   Pueblo, Colorado

Hank Basford   Paonia, California

Grover Bates   Deerfield Beach, Florida

Richard Bertoni   Ann Arbor, Michigan

Nelson Bivins   Fountaintown, Indiana

William Brackett   Butler, Pennsylvania

Lionel Bushey   Phoenix, Arizona

Wilbur Buss   Lake Elsinor, California

Earl Canfield   Anacortes, Washington

Donald Chappell   Bloomington, Wisconsin

Ed Chisa   Standish, Michigan

Lloyd Christianson   Waterloo, Iowa

Robert Cook   Hot Springs, Arkansas

Claude Corbin   Bloomfield, Indiana

David Cox   Ogden, Utah

Marion Craig   Fairview, North Carolina

Lamar Curry   Lexington, Virginia

Arthur Davenport   Big Lats, New York

Kenneth Dondero   Shorewood, Wisconsin

Dennis Doyle   Caldwell, New Jersey

Fayette Ellis   Irving, Texas

Paul Flandro   Salt Lake City, Utah

Raymond Forbus   Hugo, Oklahoma

Leonard Froncek   Gulfport, Mississippi

Donald Gilker   Loveland, Ohio

Jack Goodwin   Redding, California

Charles Grabner   Fort Wayne, Indiana

Wallace Greene Jr. Crystal City, Virginia

Ralph Haddon   Evansville, Indiana

Arlo Hansen   Ralston, Nebraska

Guy Heater, Peconic, New York

Wade Hitt   Sneads Ferry, North Carolina

Lester Hoback   Canton, Ohio

Ben Hokit   Tulsa, Oklahoma

Donald Holzer   Golden Valley, Minnesota

Paul Hopkins   West Jefferson, North Carolina

Kenneth Iverson   White Bear Lake, Minnesota

Thomas Kane   West Mifflin, Pennsylvania

Mrs. Robert Kelley   Amarillo, Texas

James Knibb   Paradise, California

Charles Klotz Roaring Spring, Pennsylvania

Anthony Kouma   Encinitis, California

Al Lavers   Colton, California

Carl Leonhardt   Morgantown, North Carolina

Pat Linder   Clear Lake, Minnesota

Frank Marshall   Lindsey, Oklahoma

Joe Martin   Henryetta, Oklahoma

Armand Masse   Lowell, Massachusetts

Richard Matthews   Fresno, California

Howard McGregor   Park Falls, Wisconsin

Leo Mickolowski   Norwich, Connecticut

William Miller   North Corona, California

Ralph Mills   Lake City, Florida

Roger Nelson   Fortuna, California

James Nethery   Bloomongton, Illinois

Stanley Nowacki   Chicago, Illinois

Faye O'Dell   Oklahoma City, Oklahoma

Robert Olson   Oregon, Wisconsin

Ellis Palm   Baudette, Wisconson

Albert Pearson   Salem, Oregon

William Pearson   Wilmington, North Carolina

James Powers   Greenfield, Massachusetts

Robert Pyle   Blaine, Minnesota

Paul Roeder   Victorville, California

Rod Sandburg   Bixby, Oklahoma

Raymond Sarazin   Esko, Minnesota

Earl Schnoeker   Steeleville, Illinois

Dodd Sellers   Tuscaloosa, Alabama

George Shell   Lexington, Virginia

Philip Spry   Concord, Michigan

William Stout   Amarillo, Texas

Milton Teske   Neenah, Wisconsin

Al Tidwell   Durrant, Oklahoma

John Tinto   Green Valley, Arizona

James Tucker   Brawley, California

Alan Tully   Lynn Haven, Florida

David Van Amburg   Yuma, Arizona

George Wilke   Rothschild, Wisconsin

James Worsley   Butler, Pennsylvania

Gavin Young   Seaside, Oregon

Edmund Youngbird   Cherokee, North Carolina

William Zachary   Pomona, California

Index

A

Adams, Corporal Hugh, 29, 35
Aerial Observers (AO) School, 22
Agerholm, PFC Harold, 98
Anderson, Corporal Jack, 77, 82, 83
Anderson, PFC Edward, 77
Aslito Airfield, 43
Autry, Gene, 4

B

Bakula, Lieutenant Walter, 51
Ball, First Sergeant Allen, 25, 49, 70
Barrows, Frederick, 97, 98
Basford, PFC Henry, 86
Bell, Staff Sergeant Lea, 68, 95
Bourke, Brigadier General, 7
Brandt, Lieutenant Jim, 3, 117
Bruce, PFC Pappy, 93
Burchfield, PFC Robert, 109
Burleigh, Lieutenant Edward, 41
Buss, Lieutenant Wilber, 2, 7, 19, 31, 42, 44, 67, 68, 98, 99

C

Camp Pendleton, 7
Camp Special Order, 17
Camp Tarawa, 6, 9, 10, 11, 12, 15, 16, 19, 21, 23
Campbell, PFCs Walter M., 77
Chappell, Donald, ix
Charan Kanoa, 36, 39, 40, 43, 45, 56
Conlon, Joseph, ix
Coop, PFC Lester, 93
Corbin, Corporal Claude, 19, 49, 50, 95, 96

Cosby, PFC Edward, 78
Coulter, PFC George, 103
Cox, Lieutenant David, 83
Crouch, Major William, 3, 44, 54, 67, 68, 89, 94, 95, 96, 99
Croxton, PFC Wilbur, 42
Curry, Brigadier General M.L., 19, 20
Czekala, Corporal Richard, 78

D

Dent, Jimmy, 76
Dent, PFC James, 74
Derose, PFC Lloyd A., 78
Dogget, Corporal Clifford, 81, 84
Dondero, Corporal Kenneth, 77, 116, 117

E

Earhart, Amelia, 49
Edmondson, Major Bob, 23
Edson, Brigadier General Mike, 25, 36
Ellis, PFC Fayette, 12, 13, 40, 81
Ener, Corporal Martin, 51
Erickson, PFC Dwain, 110
European Theater of Operations, 15
Evans, PFC Donald B., 103

F

Forsyth, Lieutenant Colonel, 48
Froncek, Corporal Leonard, 85

G

Garapan Naval Depot, 52

George Battery, 35, 49, 53, 70, 104, 107, 108, 109
Green, Lieutenant Colonel Wallace, xv, 39
Griffin, Colonel Raphael, 7, 20, 36, 44, 48
Guadalcanal, 3, 7, 15, 17, 49
Guard Force, 64
Gunty, PFC Lee, 112
Gyokusai, 58, 59, 61, 62

H

H & S Battery Marines, 29
H&S Battery, 29, 49, 73, 89, 90, 92, 96, 97, 101, 108, 117
Harakiri Gulch, 63
Hiett, Howard V., 3, 39, 48
Hight, Lieutenant Charles, 95
Hill, Rear Admiral Harry, 28
Hill, Sergeant Kenneth, 41
Hinton, PFC Everett, 87
Hitt, Major Wade, 9, 11, 9, 45, 47, 48, 108
Hobach, PFC Lester, 79, 87
Hoffman, Harold, 40, 73, 75
Hofstetter, Lieutenant, 85
Hokit, PFC Ben, 73, 75
Holzer, PFC Donald, 53, 54, 75, 84, 114
Hopkins, PFC Richard, 74
Horne, PFC Frank, 91
Hostetter, 1st Lieutenant Arnold, 73, 87, 111, 114, 116, 117
How Battery, 42, 53, 69, 71, 73, 75, 78, 80, 82, 86, 87, 89, 90, 91, 95, 101, 111, 112, 113, 115
Huston, Captain Frank, 1

I

Igeta, Brigadier General, 62
Irwin, Corporal Donald, 50
Irwin, PFC Donald, 87

J

Jensen, Mess Sergeant Alfred P., 95
Johnson, PFC Eric, 21, 81
Jones, First Lieutenant Robert, 62, 104

K

Kane, Corporal Thomas, 35
Kelly, Robert L., 28, 53, 77
Kings Theatre, 3
Klotz, Corporal Charles, 6, 47
Knibb, PFC James, 112
Kouma, Corporal Anthony, 92, 93

L

Lane, 1st Lieutenant Hal, 69
Lane, Lieutenant Hal, 50
Lane, Lieutenant Harold, 12
Lanes, Lieutenant Hal, 87, 113
Larsen, PFC Eugene, 112
Larson, PFC Swede, 85
Leonhardt, PFC Carl, 82, 83, 84, 113, 114
Lieber, PFC Harold, 78
Lowry, Corporal W. E., 20

M

MacArthur, General Douglas, 8
Magicienne Bay, 56, 57
Marine Corps (United States) ix, xv, 1, 3, 5, 7, 8, 16, 18, 22, 25, 27, 30, 33, 40, 42, 45, 49, 50, 55, 73, 76, 80
Marpi Point, 47, 68, 69, 102
Marshall, PFC Frank, 80, 112
Marusco, Private Ernie, 76
Matthews, Sergeant Richard, 50
Mauna Kea, 6, 8, 19
Mauna Loa, 6, 19
McCarthy, Major, 63, 65
McElroy, PFC Gilbert L., 11, 78
McNabb, PFC Paul, 105
Medal of Honor, Congressional 98
Mickalowski, Corporal Leo, 49, 110

Miller, Mike, ix
Miller, Corporal William, 2, 12, 81, 113, 116, 117
Mills, Corporal Ralph, 82
Mills, PFC Julian B., 82
Mitschers, Vice Admiral Marc, 56
Moretti, PFC Thomas, 50, 52
Mount Tapotchau, 48, 50, 51, 52, 57, 86, 87
Mount Tipo Pale, 48
Muellner, Corporal Cornelius, 41

N

Nabers, Corporal Bailey, 93, 95
Nelson, Captain Harold, 42, 81
Nelson, PFC Roger, 112
Nielson, Captain Carl A., 47

O

O'Brien, Lieutenant Colonel, 63
O'Dell, Corporal Ollie, 8, 19
Oba, Captain Sakae, 62
Obata, Lieutenant General Hideyoshi, 55
Odell, Ollie, 109
Olson, PFC Robert, 102, 103
Operation Memoranda, 17
Orrok, Lieutenant Richard, 44

P

Pace, Sergeant Robert, 80, 81
Palm, Corporal Ellis Oscar, 80, 81
Palmer, PFC Thomas, 6, 105
Parker Ranch, The, 6, 7, 19, 20
Parker, John Palmer, 6
Pearl Harbor, 4, 5, 30
Pearson, Lieutenant Al, 23, 40, 41, 44, 51, 52
Philips, PFC Edward L., 103
Polschuk, Sergeant Fred, 41
Porter, PFC Delbert, 29
Private Armand Masse, 75

Pyle, Robert, 97, 98

R

Radio Hill, 58
Ridley, PFC Sam, 91, 93
Rixey, Colonel, 48
Roaring Spring, 6, 47, 129
Rodenberg, PFC A., 20
Roeder, Lieutenant Paul, 101

S

Saito, Lieutenant General Yoshitsuga, 55, 57, 58, 59, 60, 61, 62, 64
Sandberg, PFC Rod, 9, 10, 39, 42, 85, 86, 87, 114, 115, 116
Sandburg, PFC Rod, 39, 116, 114, 114
Sarazin, PFC Ray, 42
Sargis, PFC Edmund, 110
Sartin, Sergeant Kenneth, 96
Sarvageau, PFC Paul M., 87, 113
Schmidt, PFC James, 83
Schoenker, Corporal Earl, 79, 80
Scott, Platoon Sergeant Michael J., 108
Sellers, PFC Dodd, 3, 4, 28, 44, 44, 69, 89, 91, 2, 93, 94
Shamboes, 61
Shell, Brigadier General George, 7, 36
Shepard, Wayne. C, 77
Sleutel, PFC George, 105
Smith, Lieutenant General H. M., 22, 34, 61
Smith, Major General Julian C, 1, 4, 6, 11, 15, 16, 20, 22, 24, 25, 34, 44, 54
Sowers, Corporal Oscar D., 104
Spry, PFC Philip, 84, 85
Staff College Foundation, ix
Stewart, Lieutenant Hoyt, 94
Stroebel, PFC George, 108
Strong, Kerry, ix

Suzuki, Colonel Eisuke, 65

T

Tanapag Plain, xiii, xv, 65, 68, 71, 101
Tarawa Boom De-Ay, 6, 10, 11, 15, 16, 21, 23
Tarawa campaign, 3, 4
Tarawa defenses, 3
Tarawa Operation, 8
Taylor, PFC Neil, 103
Tikal, PFC James, 82
Timinsky, PFC TR, 108
Timmons, PFC Max, 51, 107, 109
Tucker, PFC James, 51, 52, 53, 107, 108, 110
Tully, Captain Allan, 90

U

United States Navy, 55
USS Ormsby, 4

V

V Amphibious Corps, 22, 34

Virginia Military Institute, 7

W

Wade, PFC G., 20, 45
Wagner, PFC N., 20
Watson, General, 25, 36
Wollstadt, PFC John, 112
Wood, PFC Jack, 102, 103
Worsley, PFC James, 82
Wortman, PFC E., 20

Y

Yano, Rear Admiral, 62
Yeager, Corporal Ted, 96, 113
Young, Captain Gavin, 12, 89, 90, 91, 94, 95, 96
Youngbird, PFC Edmund, 105

Z

Zachary, PFC Bill, 107, 108, 109, 110
Zinberg, Doctor, 49, 90, 95
Zito, PFC Tony, 4, 9, 101, 102